SCREAM QUIETLY

ELIZABETH CARLSON

A TRUE STORY

SCREAM QUIETLY

A Gripping Account

of a Family

with Children

in World War II

Pleasant W rd

A Division of WINEPRESS PUBLISHING

Pleasant Word (a division of WinePress Publishing, PO Box 428, Enumclaw, WA 98022) functions only as book publisher. As such, the ultimate design, content, editorial accuracy, and views expressed or implied in this work are those of the author.

Unless otherwise noted, all Scriptures are taken from the *Holy Bible, New Living Translation*, copyright ©1996, 2004 by Tyndale Charitable Trust. Used by permission of Tyndale House Publishers, Wheaton, Illinois 60189. All rights reserved.

Scripture references marked NIV are taken from the *Holy Bible, New International Version*® NIV®. Copyright © 1973, 1978, 1984 by the International Bible Society. Used by permission of Zondervan. All rights reserved.

ISBN 13: 978-1-4141-0958-9
ISBN 10: 1-4141-0958-X
Library of Congress Catalog Card Number: 2007901120

Dedication

In this life the Lord has blessed me beyond all measure. It is with humbleness and immense gratitude that I dedicate this book to my Lord Jesus Christ.

The precious children and grandchildren that He has given me are gifts that surpass all earthly possessions.

So, to the youngest family members, Brad, Bryan, Ryan, and future children, I entrust this story, this heritage. At times this world can be violent. I want them to know that God is still in control and still cares what happens to each of His precious children.

Acknowledgments

The lonely road of writing this account has taken many years. I want to thank my dear friends Martha Darosci and Joyce Summers for joining me these last two years and for standing beside me to see it through to the end. They prayed for me as I wrote and listened to me read as each chapter was written. With their encouragement this account was completed before my time on earth was through.

I also want to thank my dear husband and my best friend, Stan, for encouraging me to tell "my story" and for not complaining when dinner was late and when I spent the hours and days secluded at the computer.

Most of all, I'd like to thank my dear mother for finally being able to share her memories and allowing me to tell our account of God's miraculous care for one ordinary family.

Table of Contents

Before You Begin

Aunt Zosia's ninetieth birthday party was really memorable. She looked so lovely in her new, peach-colored dress, but frail, more reserved, and sadder than I had ever seen her. During the meal, she sat next to her sister Wanda, my mother. I looked at them both and thought, *What an amazing pair!*

During their lifetimes they had experienced incredible contrasts. They were born into a happy Polish family, but at a very young age their father died. Their mother, Anna, struggled to feed and clothe her large family by continuing the watch repair business her husband had started. With hard work and the help of God, the family was able to stay together.

As beautiful young ladies, the daughters procured positions in the households of Polish royalty. Zosia worked as a companion to an elderly countess and Wanda as a nanny to a little girl in an aristocratic household. Both lived in beautiful mansions, wore exquisite clothing, and attended elaborate parties. Maids cared for all their needs. They vacationed by the sea and on expansive equestrian estates. The girls had access to all the best this world had to offer.

Then came World War II. Everything changed. Fathoms of change occurred between my birth in Poland in 1939 and our arrival here in America in 1951.

It wasn't until I was leaving Aunt Zosia's party that I was told she was saying her last good-byes to everyone. No additional medical treatment, no surgery, no amputations for her. She had decided to just let the Peripheral Artery Disease take its course. A few weeks later, she passed away.

I needed to be with her for her last few days on earth. She had been at my birth, the first person to see my face, hold me, and smile me into this world. So I was there as she lay dying–to sing to her, pray with her, and hold her hand.

After she died, we gathered around her body, held each other, and wept. Then we read the twenty-third Psalm, prayed, and thanked God for her life. I miss her to my very core. She was so precious to me!

Aunt Zosia is just one of the major characters in our family's history. I thank God for the years she was with us, but wish she could have helped me sort out my childhood memories, helped me understand them, and filled in some of the missing details. Whenever I asked her about the war years, she acted as if she hadn't heard me. Instead, she would turn the corner of our conversation and go directly to a new subject. She knew the answers to my questions but could not bring herself to talk about those times. Her memories of the war years went to the grave with her.

Over the years, my mother also ignored my questions. Her memories were too troubling.

My oldest brother, Romek, four years older than I, rarely spoke of our history. He would answer my questions with, "I remember, but I won't say." He is also gone. His lips are silenced forever.

My brother Danek, two years older than me, blocked out all his childhood memories. He does not recollect any of them.

I was left with horrible nightmares and memories of frightening events. I needed to sort them out, to have someone confirm that they truly happened. But no one was there to help me.

World War II was a terribly traumatic time for millions of people. The suffering was unspeakable. Our family story is just one of millions. Unfortunately, in our household, our story was kept quiet, almost as if we had something to hide, something never to be discussed. The account was to be kept tightly packed away, never brought down from the attic.

It wasn't until my mother was eighty-one years old that she began to share some of her memories. This was brought about by a trip to the emergency room. She was taken there because she had pains in her shoulder. She was admitted for observation. While in her hospital room, with a nurse at her side taking her pulse, her heart stopped. The nurse immediately called, "Code Blue." Doctors and nurses rushed in from all directions. The small room was filled with people and equipment. After several tries, Mother's heart started to beat again. It was a miracle! If this had happened at home, the outcome would have been quite different.

Mother awoke, only aware of faces surrounding her bed, looking down at her. At first she was startled, and then she asked, "What are you all doing here?" They told her what had happened, but she was reluctant to believe them. The possibility that she had just gotten another chance at life was unthinkable. The doctor finally had to show her the red marks on her chest before she would believe. She looked at the marks, realized what happened, and said, "Jesus is my friend. He always takes care of me."

One nurse told us, "She said it in such a matter-of-fact way. It was as if this was an ordinary, everyday, no surprise kind of event."

It was determined that heart bypass surgery was needed. She prayed, "Lord, if you let me live, I promise to share my memories and Your miracles. I will tell about what You did for us during

World War II. I will tell about how You were there all the time caring for us and protecting us."

She survived the surgery, and true to her word, she began to share her memories with me. At last she was able to add her factual memories to my tortured ones. At last she was able to affirm what I remembered.

When she first began recounting the stories, the memories that had been held back for so many years poured out in a torrent of words. She spoke fast and furious. We were here and there and this happened and that happened. It was such an outpouring that I would stop her and ask, "Was that in Germany or Poland? Were they Polish soldiers, German soldiers, or Russian soldiers?" Her answers were often rambling and fragmented. I was amazed, however, at the detail she included in her stories.

"There was *so* much!" she would say. "It's hard for me to put it all in order. I'm not just remembering—I am there again!"

For two years, with difficulty, she shared her memories while I wrote furiously and taped her recollections. Then she had a stroke. Her communication skills were gone. I, the child Ela in this story, was the only one left to tell this true survival story. I was left with a picture puzzle of information, her pieces as well as mine. It was my task to put them all together. I'm sure there were many missing pieces, but I had enough to accomplish our goal: to tell the story of what God had done for our family. I've known that I would be the one to record it. I've known this was my obligation since I was in high school here in America. Many times I started to write my recollections but could not continue because the memories made me physically ill.

To me, this task seemed overwhelming. I felt like a little bug that had to climb Mt. Everest. Every time I approached it, I would experience terrible aching in the pit of my stomach and feelings of horror, as if something awful would happen again. I'd wake in the night thinking about it. My first thoughts in the morning were of having to write. This went on for many years.

Once again I attempted this task. But this time was different. Several friends promised to pray for me as I wrote. I relied on our God to help me. Throughout Mother's life, her faith in God was unwavering, and it still is—even to this day. She has proven Him over and over again, and continues to trust Him completely. I can do no less!

For my mother, it was important that I keep the account true. "Don't add anything to the story," she often said. "The way our story unfolds is compelling enough; nothing needs to be added." The one thing she always stressed was that God was always there caring for each need, always protecting us in these incredible circumstances. Nothing else needed to be added.

So, the stories I'm going to tell you are about Aunt Zosia, my mother, and other family members; but more importantly the stories are a witness to God's grace and how He cared for one ordinary family. He gave us exactly what we needed, when we needed it. Because of Him we were able to survive a horrendous war, to survive against incredible odds.

Chapter 1

The Journey Begins

"I am with you always, even unto the end of the age."
—Matthew 28:20b

September 1946

"Eat your breakfast. You'll need lots of energy today," Wanda told her three young children. "We'll be walking all day long and you need to be strong."

"Mama, when we prayed today, why did you cry?" seven-year-old Ela asked as she poked at her plate of eggs.

"It's because I'm so happy," Wanda answered, not wanting her children to know the real reason and not wanting them to be anxious. "Soon we will be with your daddy. We will be together again and you will have a much better life."

"But Mama," Danek broke in, looking at his mother, "You said it would be a long time before we see our daddy. He lives far away, in England." His logical, nine-year-old mind wanted to make sure that everything was clear.

The decision to leave Poland had not been easy to make. Through the Underground, Wanda had learned that her husband was alive and living in England. He had been captured as a prisoner of war, released through a miracle of God, and eventually joined the British army. She wondered if Józef knew that they were alive or where they had settled.

Passage to England could be arranged in the British Zone of West Germany, but only for immediate family members of British military personnel. In 1946 it was illegal to travel out of Poland without documents. The consequences could be fatal. How could she get through the heavily guarded borders? Then, how could she travel through Germany without documents?

"Will it be long before we cross the ocean on that huge ship?" her older son asked excitedly. Romek, in his ten years, had never seen a real ship, but his Aunt Zosia was a great storyteller. She often entertained the children with vivid descriptions of things she had seen and experienced.

"Sweetheart, only God knows that. We don't know how He will guide us. When we get to safety, we will write to Daddy. He will come and get us. It may be a very long time or perhaps not."

Not wanting to believe that it could be a long time, Romek excitedly plunged into his next sentence. "I can't wait! The ship will be so long that I know I won't be able to run from one end to the other without getting tired. I know! I'll be safe on the ship and no one will stop me."

"I'm going to eat ice cream all day long," Danek interjected. Such an incredible opportunity had never approached him before. "I know you can ask for more, anytime you want, and it won't cost anything."

"We're going to sleep way up high in the air on a bed that's on top of another bed." Romek stopped long enough to take a breath and raise another spoon of eggs to his thin face. "I'll explore the whole ship and the captain will let me go to the front and steer the ship."

"Don't talk with your mouth full. You'll choke!" Wanda admonished.

"He has a white uniform with gold buttons," Romek continued, ignoring his mother's advice. "Aunt Zosia told me. She said that she saw a captain once. I can't wait! We're going to have so much fun!"

Wanda looked away from the table as tears filled her eyes. Her young son's excitement pushed reality to the surface. The thought of parting from her precious mother, two sisters, and baby niece descended on her like a dark shroud. A heavy lump formed in her throat.

They had gone through so much together since World War II started. They had crossed war zones and dodged bombs. They hid from the enemy in ditches, in bombed-out buildings, in a cave, and in bomb shelters. They had prayed together and fasted together. After her little niece was born, Wanda and the others packed themselves into a cold cattle car and traveled in the middle of winter without heat, food, or drink. When they ran out of diapers, they all helped dry the diapers on their own bodies. They had suffered hunger together and thanked God for a crust of bread together. They had experienced more war than anyone should, and they were always together. How could they part now? If only they could all leave Poland together.

The days ahead were uncertain. Only God could know if they would survive and escape to freedom.

"Finish your breakfast, children. We need to leave very soon." Wanda's heart became unbearably heavy and full.

Quickly, she left the room and went outside behind the house to shed a few private tears and pray for strength and guidance. She lifted her eyes to heaven and said, "Only You know, dear God, if I shall ever see my mother and sisters again on this earth. Lord, I don't want to leave them, but I feel I must—for my children. I don't know what's ahead. I don't even know which direction to travel if we are able to cross the border. I'm so scared! Please give me courage for whatever is ahead. You have preserved us so many times before. I know you will be with us now. You are my God and I trust You."

Wanda leaned against the stucco wall to compose herself before she returned to her children and gave herself permission to remember.

The summer of 1939 in Lublin, Poland, was ordinary and peaceful. Wanda had her little brood of healthy children; her husband, Józef, was earning a good living at his job. As most young couples, they had dreams, plans, and hopes for a bright future. Life was good.

Wanda's four-year-old son, Romek, was an appealing little boy with curly dark hair and defined features. With a ready smile, he greeted everyone. Everyone was his friend. He was fun to be with because of his enthusiasm, vivid imagination, and talk of the huge plans he had for what he wanted to be when he grew up.

Two-year-old Danek was a fair-haired, round-cheeked child with large eyes and long, dark eyelashes that all the women in the neighborhood envied. What a plump, round little bundle of joy!

Ela was her youngest—born in March of 1939 with only Wanda's sister Zosia present. Zosia was the only one there to help with the birth–no hospital, no doctors, no nurses. Everything went well and now Wanda felt that her family was complete.

Their apartment was on the first floor of a three story building on a street called The Third of May. Lublin was a beautiful, bustling city full of churches, cultural centers, and commerce. Miles and miles of fields and forests surrounded the city. It was an exciting place to live.

The Journey Begins

Wanda remembered the summer of 1939 as a happy time. Whenever possible, she took her children to the neighborhood park. It was beautiful! The trees and flowers and grassy places were a welcome change from the streets and houses in the neighborhood. She loved to sit on a bench and muse while her boys played in the sandbox and her infant slept in the big wicker buggy with the wicker hood and large wheels. It was hard not to enjoy those moments. She loved the beautiful blue sky, fluffy clouds, and gentle breeze as it touched the cheeks of her precious children. She was content and grateful for all God had given her.

How quickly things changed! Rumors of war started tumbling out of the shadows till they loomed over everyone like a threatening, ugly cloud. First, a notice that her husband had to immediately report to the Polish military disrupted the family.

Then he was gone—gone before arrangements could be made about what to do next.

As if by instinct, families started to gather together for comfort and safety. Zosia came to help her sister with the children; next, Wanda's mother, Anna, and her other sister, Czesia, came from the country to be with her in case the war did start. Anna had some health issues and wasn't very strong. She wanted to be with her daughters and grandchildren. She left everything behind in her apartment and only took her daughter and a few necessities.

Czesia was disabled and still lived at home with her mother. She was born with a speech impediment. At that time in Poland, no medical help was offered to special needs children. She was regarded as a mentally disabled child and was never allowed to attend school. Despite her disability, she was strong, healthy, and a hard worker but she always stood in the background because she could not express herself clearly.

Rumors of the impending war quickly became intense and everyone began to prepare. There was a buying frenzy. Quickly, everything disappeared from the shelves in the stores. All the non-perishable foods were carefully stored away in the homes. Bread was sliced and laid out on large, flat tins. These tins were taken to the baker, who put them at the back of his ovens to dry. Most households did not have ovens. Apples were peeled, cut in circles, and also dried at the bakery. Noodles were made using lots of eggs for protein. The dough was rolled out, cut, and laid out on bed sheets to dry.

During World War I, small bombs were thrown by hand from biplanes. Wanda remembered seeing them as she watched from her basement window as a child of five. During an air raid she could even see the pilot as the plane swooped low, close to the buildings. These bombs did not do a great deal of damage unless they made a direct hit. Remembering World War I, preparations were made as then.

Brown paper was cut in strips and glued to the windowpanes in a criss-cross pattern to keep the glass from shattering if a bomb should fall. Each home had two buckets by the door. One was filled with sand, the other with baking soda and water. Sand buckets with little shovels were also in the streets. The instructions were that if a bomb should fall, pour a little sand over it; when the fire is out, scoop it up with the little shovel and throw it away. They called these bombs "little golden eggs."

The other bucket in the home had water and baking soda in it. If poisonous gasses were detected, alarms would sound. Everyone was instructed to immediately dip rags into the solution and stuff the rags under the doors and in all the cracks. A wet rag was to be placed over the mouth and nose of everyone, including babies. People joked and laughed about the gas even as they heeded the false alarms. As instructed, rags, clothing, and every bit of available material was soaked in the soda water, even baby pants. One lady in the building became so excited that she soaked her fur coat and hung it over her door.

As fall approached, radio reports told of Hitler's invasion. Everyone prepared for a quick escape. Only the most precious possessions and absolute necessities were packed. At Wanda's one suitcase was filled with dried apples and another had dried bread and other food items. The baby buggy was stuffed to the brim with supplies for the children. Everything was made ready for the flight. As the invasion of Lublin became imminent, everyone slept in his or her street clothes. Some even wore shoes to bed.

Early one morning, before war had reached Lublin, there was a knock on the door. Wanda was afraid to open it. It was much too early for visitors. She peeked out the window and saw to her utter amazement that her brother Bernard, from Gdynia, was there with his bicycle in tow. Quickly, she rushed to the door and opened it. Just as quickly, he pushed his way into the apartment and closed the door. His face was ashen—his voice shaking.

"What happened to you? Why are you here? Where is Natalia and your baby? Why did you leave Gdynia?" The questions poured out as his sisters and mother gathered around him. His eyes filled with tears as he started to unweave a terrible account:

"We were sleeping in our house—it was the middle of the night. Loud banging on our door woke us. Hitler's soldiers were at our door demanding to come in. They had rifles with bayonets attached and were pointing them right at us. We were told that we had half an hour to pack and leave the house. Half an hour! This was our house. How could they tell us to leave? What can you pack in half an hour? The soldiers stayed with us while we dressed and packed." He started to sob, but still wanted to continue.

"When we came out of our house we saw that all of our neighbors were in the street. We were all packed together like sardines. They told us we were going to be relocated because the Reich needed our houses. The mothers and young children were separated from the men and boys. Natalia and the baby went with one group and I went with another. Both groups marched to the station. I took my bicycle. The soldiers demanded that I leave it behind. I told them that I needed it as a support for my injured leg. I limped profusely to show them. I really hadn't injured my leg, but I had a plan.

"At the station we were all herded into cattle cars. Natalia was taken to one train and I was put on a different one. There were so many of us in the cattle car that we could not even sit down. We had to ride like that till almost dawn. At dawn, the train stopped outside of a little town. Some of the men and boys were chosen and told to get off. They were taken to dig ditches. Whispers alluded that they were digging graves for themselves. I didn't know what to think.

"The train stopped again, this time outside of Lublin. Hope sprang into my heart. Perhaps I could manage to escape and come to you. As men were selected to get off the train, I pushed into that group. I took my bicycle. Again the soldiers objected. Again I told them about my leg. When they saw how I limped, they let me keep the bicycle.

"As we walked toward a field at the edge of the woods, I limped profusely and slowed down until I was at the end of the line. When the soldiers weren't looking, I disappeared and hid in the woods. They didn't notice that I was gone. I hid till they were all out of sight. Then I came here."

Wedding photo of Wanda and Józef.

Chapter 2

Bombing of Lublin

The Lord is my shepherd; I have everything I need. Even when I walk through the dark valley of death, I will not be afraid, for you are close beside me. Your rod and your staff protect and comfort me.

—Psalm 23:1 and 4

Even though people had prepared for war, no one could have imagined the devastation that lay ahead. Early one morning, while some were still sleeping in their beds, the threatening drone of heavy bombers could be heard in the distance.

It was just moments later that the world changed for the residents of Lublin. Bombs fell from the sky, causing torturous destruction. Exploding bombs formed huge craters all over the city–craters so large that a whole house could fit inside, and so deep they drew water. Windows shattered, spraying glass into the street and onto onlookers. Debris flew in all directions, as if the town were in the eye of a tornado.

Within moments, people were running in the streets, some partially clothed, some naked, screaming, crying, calling for help. People were bleeding. Some lay with limbs missing; some ran with flesh burning. Others were silenced forever.

Even though Wanda's family had rehearsed exactly what to do and slept fully dressed, the commotion within their household was tremendous. While bombs were falling outside, inside the apartment, Anna grabbed four-year-old Romek. Zosia took two-year-old Danek, while Wanda held Ela, her six-month-old infant girl. They all ran to the basement. Czesia followed with two suitcases and Bernard steered his baggage-laden bike into the basement.

Bombs exploded, shaking the houses and cracking foundations. Within moments it was evident that this was not the place to be. It was time to take a chance and run for the edge of town. Wanda ran back up into the apartment, put the baby into the buggy and headed out into the street. The others followed.

When all were in the street, they ran toward the edge of town. Dodging the craters, ignoring the mortally wounded, and deafening their ears to all the death cries, they ran. Like horses with blinders on, everything had to be ignored. They had to concentrate on the task at hand. On such a day, emotions had to be paralyzed, ignored, put on hold. It was time to just save those you loved. They ran to the outskirts of Lublin, east toward the woods, and away from the approaching Nazis.

Dragging the buggy through the littered street was manageable, but once they reached the potato fields, it became another matter. The uneven field and deep furrows made pulling the buggy almost impossible. Wanda considered taking the baby and leaving the buggy right in the field. But with a little reshuffling, and a little help, she continued to drag it along. Progress was slow. The little boys had to walk, tired or not. Occasionally they would get a ride on Bernard's shoulders or, for a little while, were carried.

By late afternoon they came to a small valley with patches of tall grasses. They were just too tired to continue, even though the forest beckoned in the near distance. This valley looked like a good place to stop and rest. Exhaustion and hunger compelled them to rest. As Zosia sat down, she was shocked to notice that her feet were bare. In the rush, she had forgotten to put her shoes on. She had walked on glass, around craters, and over rubble. Miraculously, not even one tiny cut appeared on her feet. Fortunately, the night before she had placed her shoes in the baby buggy. Quickly she retrieved them and laced them onto her bare feet.

No one had eaten a thing since the night before, not even the children. Everyone was famished. Wanda nursed her infant while the others eagerly waited for a little meal. It was Czesia's designated responsibility to carry the suitcase filled with bread and food. All eyes were on that precious suitcase as it was opened. To their utter dismay, the suitcase didn't have bread; it was filled with dried apples. In her haste, Czesia had taken the wrong suitcase. Dried apples were passed around. They were good, but not as filling as bread would have been.

After the apple meal, the children still complained of hunger so Bernard went out by himself to search for food. He walked at the edge of the field where the field met the woods. If a plane came, he could quickly duck into the woods and hide till it passed by.

He walked until, in the distance, he saw a farm. Everything looked peaceful there. Chickens clucked as they pecked at the ground, the cows were in the field, and the garden looked ready for picking. Everything looked normal. Approaching the farmhouse cautiously, Bernard knocked on the door. His heart pounded as he waited for someone to come. He was hoping the farmer would sell him some food, but feared who might be inside. Could this house hold the enemy, and not a farmer?

A middle-aged man came to the door. His cracked hands and furrowed face were heavily tanned from the sun, his clothing worn and dirty. Looking into the farmer's eyes Bernard asked, "Can you sell me some food? We have three small children and nothing to give them." As he spoke, he looked at the man for that glimmer of sympathy that he hoped was there.

"I'm really sorry," the farmer said. "We have had many people come by today. All I had, I have sold. This has been an awful day. My heart hurts for all of you but you are lucky, you are still alive and have made it this far."

"Please, could you look again?" Bernard begged. "I will pay you! Please, just anything to get us through the night. The children are crying and I can't bear it!"

The farmer thought for a minute, and then said, "I still have some laying chickens. Who knows if any of us will be here to see the dawn? Who knows if we will ever need the eggs? Wait here." Off to the chicken coop he went and stayed there till he returned with a fresh chicken for the pot.

"I don't have anything to cook it in," Bernard stated. "Would you be kind enough to lend me a pot? I will return with it to-night. I promise."

The kind farmer gave him the pot, a little bread and milk, and everything that he needed to cook the meal. Bernard paid the man and retraced his steps across the fields to the edge of the woods and back to the valley where his family waited.

While Bernard was gone, the family rested quietly in the long grasses. In this silence, they began to relax. Soon voices wafted across the valley. Heads quickly turned as they listened to determine from which direction the sounds were coming. Wanda climbed to the edge of the valley to observe. Near the forest, movement attracted her eyes. Were those animals? Were they horses? Who were the people? Were they soldiers? Were they Polish national? Horror gripped her as she considered that perhaps these soldiers were Nazis. Quietly she looked and listened. Within minutes she was convinced that the voices spoke the Polish language. As her eyes gazed intently into the forest, she noticed buildings tucked in between the trees. *These must be Polish troops,* she thought. *Perhaps they will provide us a night of protection.*

Down the valley she slid, back to her family. "I am convinced that Polish military are billeted within the woods," she told them. "After dark I'll go and ask if we can sleep there. Let's rest now while we can."

In spite of the fact that the ground was becoming damp, *rest* was a welcoming word. Zosia lay down with Danek stretched out on top of her. Wanda took Romek and lay as a mattress for him. Anna put Ela on her chest and kept her warm with her body heat. Czesia stayed close, guarding the luggage.

When Bernard returned and heard the news, he was relieved momentarily, but then became anxious. What if the Polish troops wanted him to join them and fight? He had to stay and help his mother and sisters. Those anxious thoughts had to be put aside for the moment. Right now he had a task to complete. After sundown he built a fire and cooked the chicken. The darkness hid the smoke and the valley hid the fire.

When the chicken was cooked, they paused to thank God for this meal and for sending His angels to protect them during this unmerciful nightmare. Silently, everyone shared in the meal. It was now dark and the danger of bombing had stopped for the day. Bernard did what he had promised. He went back to the farm to return the cooking pot, while Wanda took Ela in her arms and walked toward the woods.

Chapter 3

The Dark Valley
of Death

"For I know the plans I have for you," says the Lord. "They are plans for good and not for disaster, to give you a future and a hope."

—Jeremiah 29:11

As Bernard went to return the cooking pot, Wanda made her way to the top of the little valley. With her skirt swishing against the long grass, she proceeded to cross the field. A sliver of a moon cast a little light on the potato field and guided her way toward the woods. She was so intent on her goal that she scarcely felt the warm body of her infant snuggled up against her. By taking little Ela with her, she felt that she would have a better chance of evoking sympathy from the soldiers. How could they refuse to help a mother with a baby in her arms?

"Oh, Lord", she prayed, "You have always been with me, throughout all my life. Help me again now. We really need a warm place for the children tonight. Please help us find a safe place to sleep."

Drawing closer, even more buildings were discernible to her. She noticed Polish soldiers with rifles moving back and forth, guarding the area. Apparently, this must be a Polish military post. Would the men in charge be sympathetic and allow non-military personnel into the complex?

As Wanda approached a group of soldiers, they readied their rifles and pointed them into the darkness where she stood. With her heart pounding, slowly she moved toward them and into the light. In Polish, she said, "Do you have a corner somewhere where we can sleep? I have small children and I need some shelter for them tonight. We will be on our way again early tomorrow morning."

The men looked at her and her baby, then at each other. Lowering their rifles, they discussed the possibilities. "You can stay in that barn over there. If you need to, just move the horses to another stall and take the berth at the end of the barn. It's probably a little cleaner there."

Gratefully, she thanked them and told them she would return in a little while with the rest of her family. The soldiers agreed and back she went to the valley to rejoin her family. "I have good news! We have a place to stay tonight. The soldiers will let us sleep in the barn," she told them excitedly.

When Bernard returned he was grateful to hear the news but was concerned. He was a man. He had escaped from the Nazis. What would be next? Would they question him? Would he have to separate from the family? Immediately, he became that disabled, limping old man again. Leaning heavily onto his bicycle, with his hat pulled low over his eyebrows, he limped his way toward the compound.

Tired or not, everyone had to walk. Little Danek almost disappeared into the tall grasses. His short, two-year-old legs couldn't keep up with the adults, so Bernard propped him on the bicycle and continued pushing. Through the potato field they trudged toward the military base. Wanda led the parade pulling the buggy, Zosia followed with four-year-old Romek in tow, and Anna and Czesia came close behind. Bernard was at the tail end of the parade, struggling with the bicycle loaded with baggage and Danek on top.

When the soldiers again saw Wanda, they waved her on. She led her entourage into the barn.

Many of the stalls were filled with beautiful, aristocratic horses. They hardly lifted their majestic heads at the intruders. The odor in the barn was warm and familiar, a smell that did not offend them. Wanda loved horses and loved to be around them. As an experienced equestrian, she could ride like the wind. She had spent many happy hours riding on an expansive estate while working for Polish aristocracy. Tonight, this barn was a warm and welcoming place.

At the rear of the building was a birthing pen. The straw was sweet, as if it had been freshly harvested. A home away from home was made in this straw-strewn corner and everyone settled in for some sleep. All, that is, except Wanda. She could not sleep, so she sat and prayed. Into the night she talked with God. She would doze a little, then wake and pray again.

Early in the morning, while it was still dark, Wanda heard commotion outside. Getting up from her warm corner, she walked through the barn to the front door. There she stood and observed soldiers rushing around in the courtyard. Something was wrong! She stood in the doorway and kept watching and listening. A soldier ran up to her and excitedly said, "Lady, get out of here. This is an ammunition storage area and the Germans have discovered us. Their planes will be here at dawn. Hurry! We're going to be bombed!"

Another soldier ran to Wanda and said, "Get going, but don't walk along the road or they will shoot you."

Within moments, the family was outside again, powered by adrenaline, pushing against the dirt mounds in the field, rushing to get away. Trekking through the potato fields with a buggy was almost an insurmountable task. Was it really worth keeping it? Again, Wanda considered leaving the buggy behind, but the children needed all the items in it and the baby needed a spot to sleep. She kept on dragging the buggy with Zosia and Czesia helping with an occasional push. Progress was slow.

As the morning light started to appear, with it came the dull drone of the approaching bombers. Quickly, the adults dropped to the ground, hiding the children beneath their bodies. Right there in a rocky ditch in the field, the adults shielded the children. If a bullet should target them, they thought perhaps the children would survive. Within moments the planes were overhead, vibrating the land and everyone on it to their very core. Wanda's family waited—waited to die.

As if in slow motion, bombs fell onto the military base. The huge explosions and engulfing flames shot into the sky as if it were a pulsating, raging inferno. The whole countryside churned and was engulfed in flames. This explosion was even more powerful and destructive than the bombing they had experienced the day before in Lublin.

A few minutes later, another group of planes arrived and bombed the rest of the compound. Anything that was still standing was targeted.

In the ditch, nobody moved. The children, still sheltered by the adults, stayed quiet. Everyone waited.

As the inferno blazed, billowing smoke drifted across the sky. The breeze kept blowing, the grass and trees were still there, the plowed field was still in place, and this family still crouched, waiting and waiting.

Each time it appeared to be safe to move, the rumble of the planes would be heard again. And each time, Wanda's family, still in the rock-filled ditch, lay frozen with fear. The Nazi planes came closer and closer and started to circle overhead. As if the devastation was not sufficient, they now proceeded to shoot anything that moved. The machine gun rampage overpowered all sounds. Poor defenseless people, walking along the road, were shot dead and strewn along the road like so much chord wood that had spilled from a logging truck. Most of the victims were women and children.

What carnage! How could anyone watch this and not scream to heaven? These were innocent people. What did they do to deserve this? Who did they harm? They were just looking for safety.

Wanda's family stayed in the ditch, safe.

Chapter 4

The Enemy Has Chased Me

My enemy has chased me. He has knocked me to the ground. He forces me to live in darkness like those in the grave. I remember the days of old. I ponder all your great works. I think about what you have done. I reach out for you. I thirst for you as parched land thirsts for rain. Let me hear of your unfailing love to me in the morning, for I am trusting you. Show me where to walk, for I have come to you in prayer.

—Psalm 143:3, 5, 6, and 8

As the family rose from the ditch, it was impossible to ignore the wounded and dying. The adults were pulled between running to the road to help the wounded and running to the woods to survive. What should they do? Scores of people were shot and lay motionless all along the road. Were they all dead? Wanda's family had the children to protect. So they ran to the woods.

Movement through the woods—pulling the buggy, pushing the bicycle, holding the children's hands—was tortuously slow. Everyone had to walk, even the little boys. At a small child's pace they pushed on. All day long they walked. Many times they were forced to rest. Two-year-old Danek would walk, then ride on the bike, then ride in the buggy with the baby on top of him, and then walk again. Four-year-old Romek kept trudging on, hardly acting like a child, trying to keep up with the adults. How could a child remain a child in such circumstances? Today, everyone had been changed–forever.

It was midafternoon by the time they came to a neatly landscaped farm with fruit trees surrounding the farmhouse. This was not an ordinary farm. The building was made of brick, the trim neatly painted, and the roof was red tile. Most farmers could not afford that kind of roof. Most farms had thatched roofs and humble surroundings.

As they approached, a chained dog began to bark. The man of the house came out to investigate. "Can you sell us some food?" Wanda pleaded.

"We have sold almost all we can spare," the farmer said. "We have our own large family to feed." But when he saw the children and the exhausted family, he took pity. "You'd better come in. It's not safe to stay outside. Come in and rest for a while." The farmer released the dog and the dog joined them as they went inside.

It was wonderful to feel the safety and warmth of a home again. Here were walls, a door, windows, and a roof. Seeing this family gathered around the large kitchen table with a dog milling underfoot made the world feel almost "normal" again. Several children and an older couple sat around the table. The farmer pulled his wife aside and, looking away, whispered something to her. Immediately the wife motioned to the family. "You have such young children. We will sell you a little food. Come and sit down."

Food being prepared! What a beautiful sight! The woman scrambled some eggs and brought milk, bread, and even butter to the table for everyone, the adults included. What a banquet! What a surprising, unbelievable banquet! Quietly, Wanda's family bowed their heads and thanked God for this generous family and for the wonderful meal. They ate the food with such zest that in a few minutes the farmer's wife provided even more food. She heated some soup and mashed potatoes and said, "I can't cook much because the Nazis will see the smoke from our chimney."

This was amazing, far more then they had expected. What a privilege it was to be in this home. *Wouldn't it be wonderful if we could stay here tonight?* Wanda thought.

After the meal, the farmer's children gathered Romek and Danek and together they played with the dog. As they were petting him, the dog froze, started to shake and whimper, and then slithered away. He ran toward the window and hid in the curtains. Immediately, everyone realized why. The whining of the planes in the distance predicted the worst. Everyone dashed into hiding; some hid under the kitchen table, others under windows, and some in the hall. Wanda took her three children and pulled them all into one corner. *If we die, then we will die together,* she thought.

Within moments, the planes were overhead and machine-gun bullets sprayed the building. Bullets shattered the roof tiles and they came bouncing down the roof with a terrible clatter. Wanda felt like the tiles were landing on her head and traveling down her spine. She crouched lower and tightly held her children.

When the planes were gone, everyone came out of hiding. The house and roof were badly damaged, but no one was hurt.

"You can't leave now. It's too dangerous," the farmer's wife said. "Stay here tonight. You can leave in the morning."

Another nightmare of a day was over. Again, the family survived. Wanda tried to sleep, but her mind was racing. *Will tomorrow be better?* she wondered. *At least the night will be quiet. The planes will not come during the night. But where can we get away from this? Where, Father, where?*

Morning came too quickly. It was time to go. After another morsel of bread and milk, the family paid the farmer and departed.

Another beautiful September morning had dawned, just as it had thousands of times before. Other times it would have been a day for laughing, playing, working, and doing the normal things of life, but today would be a day of trying to survive.

They trudged through the woods, then through the fields, and even along a narrow road that edged the woods. Their ears and nerves were tuned to the foreboding drone of the hideous planes. If they heard them, they dashed into the woods and hid.

Again, progress was slow–rest time for the boys, nursing time for the baby, and dried apple eating time for everyone. Without a definite destination it was hard to press forward.

By early evening the sun gave hints of the night to come–time to look for shelter. In the distance, an obviously abandoned house was spotted. It was the only house in view but very close to the edge of the road. Could they take a chance and rest there?

As they expected, the house had been bombed. Part of it was still standing, but all the windows were shattered, the door was missing, and shards of burned timber stood pointing to the sky. Every piece of furniture was gone. Just burned-out remnants remained. Nevertheless, for lack of a better place, this would be home for the night. Bernard and the women busied themselves looking for any leftover food, unburned blankets, or anything else that could make the night more comfortable. Nothing of substance was found, just some tattered rags. They were better than the damp, cold ground. So in a corner they placed the gathered rags on the floor, and settled down for the night.

Chapter 5

The Journey Continues

Don't be afraid, for I am with you. Do not be dismayed, for I am your God. I will strengthen you. I will help you. I will uphold you with my victorious right hand.

—Isaiah 41:10

The night was long and damp, and the adults were restless. On the rags the children slept peacefully as if in their own beds. How innocent they looked, deep in their sleep, not fearing anything, trusting, just as all children should. This bombed-out house was a sanctuary for the whole family. They were grateful to be together and to be alive.

Before dawn, Wanda heard something in the distance. Did a dream wake her? Her mind immediately became alert. Quietly, she inched her way to the shattered window. In the distance she saw shadows. She listened. Her eyes were fixed on the shadows and the surrounding landscape. The shadows were moving. They came closer and closer.

Czesia lifted her head and whispered, "What's there?"

"I don't know," Wanda answered.

Quietly, Czesia crept towards the window and crouched beside her sister. Together, they observed.

The shadows turned into silhouettes and the silhouettes into people. A group of people shuffled slowly along the road. They looked exhausted, rather ordinary, just like Wanda's own family. But why were they walking toward them? Instead of walking away from the big city, they were walking toward Lublin. Were they lost? The group looked ragged and drained and walked as if all hope was gone. She could hear them talking. They were talking in the Polish language. As they came closer, Wanda came out of hiding and asked, "What's happening? Are you lost? Why are you walking towards Lublin?"

"Everywhere we go there is bombing and death. We can just as well die in Lublin as anywhere else. We're going back," they said flatly as they continued walking.

Going back to what? Wanda thought. *Will anything be left to go back to?* But where else could they go? they said. They had to at least see what was left of Lublin.

Among the rags, Wanda sat with her family and discussed what they should do next.

A small village called Siedliszcze was about sixty kilometers west of Lublin. Good friends of theirs lived near that village. Surely they would welcome them and invite them to wait out the rest of the war together. A small village certainly must be safe. Why would artillery be wasted on a small village? The only way to get there was by foot. No form of transportation was available. Walking with small boys and an infant would be very difficult, but what choices were there? A trip like this could take days or even longer. Only God would know if this was even possible.

All agreed on the following plan: They would return to Lublin and see what was left. If their apartment building was still standing and if their belongings were still salvageable, they would re-pack, rest, and leave again. But now, they would walk back as far as possible, but this time in the woods. In the afternoon, they would sleep in the woods and then walk on the road at night.

The Journey Continues

Within a few minutes Wanda's family headed for the woods and started the walk back to Lublin.

Tucked safely away among the tall, cool pines, they felt safe. The canopy of branches sheltered them as they struggled between the trees, through the underbrush, and over fallen trees. In a happier time, many hours were spent there gathering mushrooms. These little prizes would be taken home, threaded on a string, and hung next to the stove to dry. They almost were regarded as gold. Dried mushrooms added such a rich depth of flavor to many, many delicious meals.

This morning, however, the only stops were to rest, nurse the baby, and eat some dried apples. By afternoon, they were ready to sleep and wait till dark.

The road was even and straight, and at night, the moon gave just enough light to safely walk. Progress was much faster. In this way they walked and slept until they reached the outskirts of Lublin.

Before the sun rose, the edge of the city was in sight. Darkness could not hide the torment that was still in the streets. Bombed-out buildings were smoldering. Destruction was everywhere. All the bodies had not yet been collected. Since the initial bombing, not much had changed.

Returning to the devastation was nearly more than Wanda's family could endure. Where could they go to avoid these sights? The need for rest, food, and reorganization drove them onward with senseless hope. What if soldiers were occupying their home? What if the apartment wasn't even there anymore? They continued picking their way through the streets.

Just as the sun was rising, with great anticipation they reached their neighborhood. Drawing closer, hope sprang within them. Some of the buildings were still standing. Could it be that God had protected their little corner of the world? Could it be that their apartment was still habitable? Peering down the street, buildings were silhouetted against the sky. As they came closer, they saw a building that looked like their apartment building! Was it their home? It was difficult to orient oneself with so many of the landmarks missing. Their pace quickened. With hope they walked down the street. There was their building. It was still standing! Their apartment was still there!

Eagerly, they entered the apartment building and looked. The door to their home stood wide open, exposing everything inside. In haste to escape, no one had even thought to close the door. Looking around, amazingly everything looked in order. Against the wall stood the suitcase with the dried bread and foodstuff. The beds were disheveled. In fact, everything was exactly as it had been left the moment they escaped. To their relief, nothing was missing. In fact, *nothing* had even been touched. Miraculously, even the windows were intact.

Quickly, they locked the door and busied themselves with getting a meal, putting the children to bed, re-packing and resting. They relished the roof, the walls, the unbroken windows, and the surroundings of their home. Resting in a bed felt like heaven, especially since they did not know when they might be sleeping in a bed again.

By early evening, the reorganized packages were tied to the bicycle and preparations were made to leave. This time the buggy and many of the other items were left behind. Just a few bundles were taken. They were ready. But before leaving, they gathered close together, as was their custom, embraced each other, and tearfully prayed. "Dear God, You have been so good to us. You have preserved us in this unspeakable time. Thank You for hearing our prayers. Thank You for being with us. Thank you for being our God. Please, Lord, grant us safety again as we leave. We need wisdom from You. Show us what to do and where to go."

When they had finished praying, they locked the door tightly behind them, and walked out onto the street and into their destiny.

Chapter 6

Walking Through Fire

When you walk through the fire, you will not be burned;
the flames will not set you ablaze. For I am the LORD, your
God, the Holy One of Israel, your Savior.

—Isaiah 43:2b and 3a NIV

If you make the Lord your refuge, if you make the Most High
your shelter, no evil will conquer you; no plague will come
near your dwelling. For he orders his angels to protect you
wherever you go.

—Psalm 91:9–11

The sixty-kilometer walk to Siedliszcze had begun. The next
few days would be hard, but at least this family now had a
destination. Bernard always had been strong and felt he could
manage pushing the package-laden bicycle, but getting through
the streets of bombed-out Lublin, with soldiers on guard, was
the first obstacle. A curfew was in effect and no one was allowed
outside after dark. This made it urgent to be out of sight and
off the streets quickly.

Pretending to be severely disabled, Bernard limped and
shuffled along like a very old man. The events of the last few
days had left him physically and mentally exhausted. So much

had happened. He had lost his wife, his child, his house, his possessions, his neighbors, his work, and everything that was familiar. With a broken spirit, he indeed looked like an old crippled man.

The evening was still young. A multitude of armed soldiers guarded detainees who were removing rubble and gathering up remnants of the dead. Bernard had to be strong. His mother, sisters, and the children all depended on him. He had to help them reach safety. Pulling his hat even farther over his brow, he continued hobbling along, pushing his bicycle through town. Fortunately, the military was too occupied to pay attention to another group of unfortunates walking the streets.

Once Wanda's family reached the edge of town and entered the fields, they felt a little better, a little safer, a little braver. Acres of potato and sugar beet fields stretched out in front of them. This was a welcoming sight after leaving the devastation within the city. Here, things looked normal. Plants were still growing, birds were still flying looking for the last morsel of the day, and the sun was starting to set. These fields had to be crossed before the safety of the forest would surround them.

Even without the buggy, progress was difficult. The bicycle laden with packages did not hold everything. Everyone had something to carry. Staunch little four-year-old Romek could not walk as fast as the adults, but he tried. Somehow, he didn't complain. This child had already been changed by this war. He understood what was at stake and did not behave as a typical youngster. He did, however, tire more quickly than the adults. Czesia, Zosia, and Wanda would occasionally give him a ride on their shoulders, but mostly he walked. Two-year-old Danek wanted to be carried, but even he had to walk his share, tired or not. Baby Ela was shuffled among the arms of whoever had the strength.

With visions of being welcomed by their friends in Siedliszcze they pushed on. Through the still-growing sugar beet field, through the potato fields, and through the woods they walked. Whenever possible they walked on the road, always with a listening ear for that awful drone of the killing planes. If planes were heard, everyone automatically dove between the sugar beets or in the ruts of the potato fields, hiding the children under the adults' bodies. There they stayed, without moving, until the planes passed and disappeared. If they were close to the woods, they would run and take shelter beneath the trees.

When exhaustion took its toll, sleep came quickly in a dry, rock-filled ditch. The children were again tucked in for the night on top of the warm bodies of the adults. Slumber could only last a few hours. The journey had to go on.

During the night, the walking became easier. Walking on the desolate country roads felt safe. Soldiers were not around and planes did not fly at night. The bicycle glided almost effortlessly over the road at night, compared to the many hours of struggling through the fields and woods during the day.

For three days and nights they trudged along, sleeping during the day or at night in ditches, on rocks, on the ground, in the forest, or whenever exhaustion overtook them. Wherever they walked, the road was always kept in sight so that they would not get lost.

In the late afternoon of the third day, new energy filled the travelers. They were almost there. Siedliszcze was only a couple of kilometers away. Wanda remembered that the only way to reach the village was to cross a bridge built of heavy timbers. She remembered the beautiful setting. Grass covered the countryside, sheep strolled the rolling hills, and wildflowers grew everywhere. The bridge spanned a deep ravine that cradled the Wieprz River. Once over the bridge, the road turned to lead the way to a picturesque water mill. Farmers would bring grain to be ground into flour. The scene was breathtaking, like a beautiful painting.

On this September day, it was equally breathtaking, but something was different. As they drew closer, horror seized them. The bridge had been bombed and the timbers were still burning. Why? Why here? Why was this desolate place bombed?

As they looked at the bridge they could see huge gaps in the timbers with planks missing. Those that were left were charred and still burning with a hot fire. The whole structure looked foreboding and dangerous. What could they do now? This was the only way to the village. Walking to the next bridge, if there was even one left, could take another day. The children were tired. They had to do something.

"I'll try to go across," Bernard offered. "If the beams can support me, then the rest of you will be able to cross." Gingerly, he wove his way across the burning bridge. It did not collapse. The heat singed the hair on his arms, but he was able to cross over the river. Quickly, he returned for his bicycle and then, one by one, escorted the others across the bridge.

Chapter 7

Showing Love in Wartime

Most important of all, continue to show deep love for each
other, for love covers a multitude of sins. Cheerfully share
your home with those who need a meal or a place to stay.
God has given gifts to each of you from his great variety of
spiritual gifts. Manage them well so that God's generosity
can flow through you.

—1 Peter 4:8–10

Quickening their pace, within minutes they arrived at the home
of their good friends. Even though a bombed-out bridge had
just been crossed, they knew that at last safety would surround
them.

Mr. and Mrs. Plitczek's farm was modest, but nice. The
pleasant thatched-roof cottage beckoned them. Cows grazed
contentedly in the surrounding pastures while chickens pecked
away under the trees in the orchard. A well-kept garden still
produced food.

With open arms, the Plitczeks welcomed Wanda and her
family. What joy it was to at last be in their home, to at last be
surrounded by love, warmth, and safety. After many hugs and
kisses, everyone was ushered into the bright kitchen with the

whitewashed wall. To their utter surprise, sitting at the table were their long-time friends from Lublin, Mr. and Mrs. Pitts. What excitement to see them and to be together! They had also walked from Lublin, but never once had their paths met.

Over the years, many happy times had been shared with Mr. and Mrs. Pitts. Both of them were jovial folks who loved to laugh and entertain guests. Anna had known them since her youth and always enjoyed visiting with them. They were senior citizens and now were rather heavy-set but in good health. Mr. Pitts, however, had a challenge. He only had one leg. While he was still young, he lost it in an accident and now wore a prosthetic.

After heartfelt greetings, it was obvious that something was wrong, terribly wrong. Wanda had never seen them so sullen and sad.

There was so much to catch up on, but right now, exhaustion spoke loudest. Food and sleep were first on the agenda. Tomorrow they would talk. After three days of walking without being able to take shelter beneath a roof, primary needs had to be met. Everyone longed to stretch out and finally rest.

Seeing the need, Mrs. Plitczek immediately fed everyone and busied herself looking for bedding. She made comfortable beds on the floor. Without fussing, the children quickly fell asleep. Zosia, Czesia, and Wanda joined the children and were grateful to at last be able to sleep under a blanket. Mr. and Mrs. Pitts slept in a spare room while Anna retired on a daybed in the kitchen. Bernard slept on the floor close to the front door. The house was full, but accommodated everyone.

It was good to have a place to sleep, but sleep was fitful for the overtired Wanda. She would wake every few minutes, listen, go to the window, look out, and then lay back down again.

During the night she heard rumbling. At first it sounded like a soft vibration in the distance. The vibrations became louder and louder until they sounded like heavy machinery approaching.

Nervously, she jumped up and again looked out of the window. To her horror, headlights from a convoy of tanks were heading directly toward the house. The tanks were so close that the lights were almost shining into the window.

"Wake up!" she yelled. "Tanks are coming! Wake up!" she shook everyone and dragged the children toward the door.

Everyone was fully dressed except for Mr. Pitts. He had taken his leg off and was hopping around in a panic, trying to put it back on again. He hopped and hopped around in his long underwear and was unable to attach his leg.

As they were ready to dash out the door, Wanda again glanced out the window. "They've turned off their light!" she whispered in horror.

With pounding heart, she looked again. The tanks were gone. A natural curve in the road had made it appear as if they were coming directly at the house, but as the road turned, the tanks passed right beside the farm and continued down the road. Even though danger had passed for now, why were the tanks in the area? Where were they going in the middle of the night?

When Wanda woke early the next morning, Mr. Plitczek had already made a fire in the stove and had gone out to milk the cows and feed the chickens. Dear Mrs. Plitczek was quietly making a big batch of bread dough. Anna woke, but Mrs. Plitczek encouraged her to stay in bed. What generous, wonderful people! They were willing to share all that they had.

Before long everyone was stirring and another day had begun. Zosia and Czesia helped prepare the breakfast. Pancakes were made using lots of eggs. They would be served with jam, tea, and milk! What an incredible meal!

Wanda busied herself caring for her baby and then the diaper laundry. Bernard went to the barn to help Mr. Plitczek.

When the breakfast was ready, the whole group, nine adults and three children, gathered in the kitchen, thanked God for providing so generously, and shared the delicious meal.

Much had to be accomplished during the day. No one had bathed or changed clothes in many days. Baths would be first. Water was brought in from the outside pump and heated on the stove. Cold water was poured into the corrugated metal tub placed on the kitchen floor. Just enough hot water was added to make a comfortable bathing temperature. The children were washed first. For privacy, blankets were held up as one by one the adult family members took their turn in the same water. What a privilege to be clean again!

After a lunch of bread and butter, the adults sat around the table and talked. Wanda's family was anxious to hear what had happened to the Pitts. Why were they so distressed?

Chapter 8

Safely Hidden

The Lord is my light and my salvation, so why should I be afraid? The Lord protects me from danger, so why should I tremble?

When evil people come to destroy me, when my enemies and foes attack me, they will stumble and fall. Though a mighty army surrounds me, my heart will know no fear.

—Psalm 27:1–3

As the bread dough was rising, the friends sat around the table sharing the common bonds that bound them–war, survival, and a mutual enemy. The hunger pangs were gone. Mrs. Plitszek's hard black bread filled the empty spaces and helped them all relax. It didn't matter that the bread was several days old. Warm milk poured over the dry bread was put in front of the little boys. She even found a little sugar to sprinkle over the bread. They ate it eagerly. Hunger is not pretentious. Gathered together, they shared experiences and anxiously waited to hear what had happened to Mr. and Mrs. Pitts.

"When the bombing started," Mr. Pitts initiated, "we both ran to the basement." He cleared his throat while Mrs. Pitts started to cry softly. Slowly, he continued. "Our son, Tadeusz, left early for work so he wasn't with us. When the bombing started, the noise was so horrendous that I thought the world was coming to an end. The bombs continued for hours. I don't know how they missed us. We should have died. People were dying all around us. It was like a hell. Rubble piled up against our entire door. We couldn't get out. We stayed in the basement for a day and a half.

"After we managed to dig ourselves out, we ran for the woods and then to the farm where Tadeusz worked. We saw him. In the field we saw him. He was there with many others." Covering her face with her apron, Mrs. Pitts started to weep inconsolably. Mr. Pitts put his arm around his wife and continued. "Our only son was shot dead. We saw him. With our own eyes we saw him. He was shot dead by the Nazis! Mother laid down on the ground beside him! She didn't want to leave. She wanted to stay there and die!

"We heard the planes again. We had to hurry and take cover or be shot beside him. She didn't want to go. I told her there was nothing we could do for him now. He would want us to save ourselves. We couldn't even stop to bury him...he was such a good son." Mr. Pitt's voice had softened to a whisper. He paused momentarily, then added, "That's when we escaped and made our way here."

What do you say to someone who has seen such a massacre and suffered such an unspeakable loss? For a few moments, everyone sat in silence. Then they went over to the Pittses and embraced them as they expressed their sympathy. Then they remembered and talked of happy times spent with Tadeusz.

"Do you remember when Tadeusz grew those wonderful green butter beans?" Wanda said. "I think they were the best that I have ever tasted. The pods were about a foot long but very tender." What ordinary talk for such an extraordinary time.

"Where did he get the seeds? What kind of fertilizer did he use?" Wanda queried. "I remember when you cooked some for us. You put butter on them and we all had a feast. Do you remember? They were wonderful!"

What she didn't say was that she had never, ever seen anyone eat more beans than Mrs. Pitts. She would take a huge bowl of those beans, eat all of them, and then fill up her bowl again. She would eat and eat those beans as her visitors' eyes got bigger and bigger with amazement.

Talking was cut short. A lot more work was ahead. Clothes had to be washed, supper had to be cooked, and the children had to be tended to. Everyone helped. Wiping her eyes with her apron, Mrs. Pitts joined in the ordinary rituals of life.

Supper was delicious, a luxurious meal. Chicken dumpling soup, fresh baked bread, milk, and tea. No one rushed, they just ate and savored each bite. In the middle of the meal, without warning, bone-chilling, whistling sounds were heard over the house. Huge explosions in the nearby field followed. Immediately, artillery shells started to fly from both directions.

"Oh, no, dear God! Not again!" Wanda cried. They had come all this way for safety and instead had landed in the middle of crossfire.

"Follow me! Quickly!" Mrs. Plitczek barked as she dashed out the door and into the yard.

Quick as a flash, everyone ran, following her to the edge of the orchard. She led the way while Mr. Plitczek pushed the others along till they reached a bushy, overgrown area with tall weeds. Mrs. Plitczek dove into the weeds and held them apart so the others could follow. Without hesitation, they all disappeared into the weeds.

Where were they? What was this? They looked around as their eyes adjusted to the dim light. Was this a cave? Yes, it was! A huge cave! Years ago, limestone was excavated by hand from this cave. A church was built nearby using this stone. Now the entrance had disappeared from view, hidden completely by the heavy underbrush.

The Plitczeks had prepared this place as a bunker for themselves. There was plenty of straw strewn in big piles and a few supplies. This hideout was supplied for just the two of them, not for a group of twelve. For now, at least, they were all safe. Somehow they would manage. The relentless crossfire continued as the Polish tanks tried to hold off the Nazis' advances. Who could have imagined that a war front would occur in this peaceful village?

In the dark cave, the group settled in on the straw. As shells thundered overhead, Wanda gathered her children close to her side. Throughout the night the bright arrows of light and blasting explosions continued. Sleep was difficult or nonexistent. The shelling continued into the next day. No one dared return to the house for more supplies or food. The warm, half-eaten meal was only a memory as they tried to sustain themselves on the meager rations in the cave.

This final stress was too much for Wanda's body. The stressful days of trying to escape the war, and the lack of food, drink, and proper rest, took its effect. She could no longer nurse her baby. There was no milk for her infant. She only could offer her water to drink. If only she could go and milk the cows! When the shelling started, the cows had scattered. Even if they were in the fields, still alive, it was too dangerous to leave the cave.

For the next three days, baby Ela had only water to drink. Even so, she did not cry. With tears in her eyes, Anna gently rocked her little grandchild. "Look at my angel," she said. "She is smiling. She does not cry."

Anna handed Ela to Zosia, found a private corner of the cave, and wept. Wanda, in another dark corner of the cave, also wept and prayed for her infant. "Lord, I have nothing to give her. Please watch over her." Talking to Jesus always gave her comfort. He had answered her prayers continually. She knew everything would be all right. Wanda wiped her eyes and returned to the family.

The shelling continued and it was still impossible to leave the cave. She gave Ela more water to drink. The baby smiled.

To soothe the boys, Wanda whispered stories into their ears. "When I was a little girl," she said, "I loved to run and play just like you do. I played with my dog, Mikuś, and all my friends in the neighborhood. You will be able to play again some day soon.

"I especially loved to run to my grandmother's and grandfather's house. They lived in the forest not too far from our house. I would run down a path, through the woods, right to their house. When I got there, the first thing I would do was kiss Grandmother's hand, then she would give me a big sugar cookie and milk. We would sit at the table together and talk about all sorts of things. I loved to go to their house. It was always such fun!

"My grandfather was a woodsman. He took care of the forest for a very rich man. The man had a great big house near Grandfather's little house. The rich man had lots of servants and horses and dogs and other animals. He was very kind to my grandparents.

"Grandfather dug a great big pond for him. This pond was filled with fishies. They were for the people who lived in the great big house. Sometimes Grandfather would let me go to this pond to get some fishies.

"First I would take my shoes off. Then I would step into the water. Then I would scoop up the fishies with my apron. They would wiggle and waggle and wiggle around." Wanda tickled the boy's tummies as she told the story. This made them laugh and wiggle too. It was hard for the boys to be still and keep silent for such a long time. The cave was dark and musty and hardly a place for little children. Wanda longed to take them out for some fresh air.

"Mama, can we ever go outside again?" Romek asked.

"We will. You'll see. We will," she promised. By morning, silence fell on the landscape. Was the shelling over? They all waited and listened; still, no shelling. The quiet in the cave was almost deafening. Wanda breathed a sigh of relief.

The sun was brightly shining on an extraordinarily beautiful September day. Danek was fast asleep, cuddled on a blanket on top of the prickly straw. Romek sat dejected. With nothing to do but twirl the straw and watch for bugs and mice, he looked very sad.

Wanda took pity on her four-year-old. What if she would take him out into the fresh air for just a few minutes?

"Romek, come here," she beckoned. "We'll go out for just a little while." Excitedly, Romek took her hand and followed her through the underbrush, into the orchard. Once out in the fresh air and sunshine, it seemed like another world. A world they once knew. Together, they quickly walked to the house, gathering up some food and a pot of water. Out the door they went, across the yard, back toward the orchard.

Without warning, the deafening sound of mortar fire whizzed over their heads. Wanda dove at her child, pushing him down onto the ground and covering him with her body. The water spilled and the food flew in all directions. Five more mortars flew over them. Leaving everything behind, they dashed back into the cave.

Chapter 9

Walking Through Death

But I am trusting you, O Lord, saying, "You are my God!"
My future is in your hands. Rescue me from those who hunt
me down relentlessly. Let your favor shine on your servant.
In your unfailing love, save me.

—Psalm 31:14–16

Once they were back inside the cave, safely tucked behind the
thick weeds, it took some time for Wanda's heart to stop racing
and her body to stop shaking. They were both safe again. The
family was together again. No one was hurt.

The hours quietly slid by and soon the crisp night air filtered into the cave. Wanda tucked the blankets tighter over her
children. The night was quiet. Several hours earlier the shelling
had stopped.

Mr. and Mrs. Plitczek took courage. With the cover of night,
both crept back to the house to get more provisions. Once inside,
they quietly turned on the radio. Listening, they could hardly
believe their ears. Could it be true? Was what they heard true
or was the enemy trying to mislead them? They went back to
the cave and shared the news.

With excitement in his voice, Mr. Plitczek said, "The radio announced that the bombing is over and everyone can return home. But let's stay here a little longer. Tomorrow I'll go back to the house and listen again. We'll see if this is true."

They had just endured three days of shelling. A few more hours in the cave wouldn't make that much difference. With the extra supplies and food, everyone was more comfortable. Almost everyone, that is, except the baby. Wanda still could not nurse her child.

"Don't worry, I'll be right back," Mr. Plitczek said as he crept out into the night. In about an hour, he returned with his arms full. In one arm he carried wood and a cooking pot. In the other he carefully held a bucket of milk.

"I thought so! One of our cows was still alive," he said. "She had returned to the barn, begging to be milked. I thought I heard her."

At the back of the cave a fire was built and the milk was boiled. At last there was some nourishment for baby Ela.

The next day, Mr. Plitczek returned to the house and the radio. What he had heard was indeed true. People were now returning to their towns and villages. The bombing and shelling had stopped.

It didn't take long for the group to gather up their belongings, thank their dear friends, and leave.

The entourage, Wanda and her three children; her mother, Anna; and her siblings, Zosia, Czesia, and Bernard; started backtracking to Lublin. Where else could they go? Perhaps life could be lived there for a while. The walk this time would be easier because they planned to walk only along the main highway.

The first few hours of the journey were almost pleasant. The fresh air and sunshine warmed the countryside and the birds flew around, enjoying the day. The grass was still green and the trees still had their leaves. The countryside looked serene. Before long they reached the highway and joined other travelers. The companionship and common purpose helped them all keep pushing toward their goal.

The highway was straight and smooth with fields on either side. It was so much easier to walk there than through the woods and fields. With renewed zeal, Bernard pushed the package-laden bicycle.

Very quickly, everything changed. Something was wrong, terribly wrong. First, a dreadful stench reached their nostrils. Then, as they drew closer, in the distance they saw that objects were strewn on the road. Quickly these objects turned into unspeakable lament before their eyes.

Along the road, in the ditches and surrounding fields were bodies–dead bodies–of women, children, and old men. Some of the dead were piled up along the sides of the road with their packages and suitcases and carts scattered in all directions. Some were covered with straw or boards, but mostly with their own coats. Some were not covered at all. All were waiting to be gathered up and buried.

"Oh, my God," Wanda cried. "This could have been our family. Dear God, why were we spared?"

"Children, don't look! Close your eyes!" the adults admonished. Walking past this atrocity while at the same time trying to hold on to the children and the packages and keep from weeping was almost impossible. The terrible stench of the decaying bodies was impossible to escape. Bernard, Anna, Zosia, Czesia, and Wanda all walked through this heavy shroud of decay. They braced themselves and numbed themselves to what they were seeing. How else could they survive without losing their minds?

Romek obediently closed his eyes and was led past the decaying bodies. Little Danek smelled the air filled with death. Baby Ela also breathed in this stench. They all walked as quickly as they could but could not escape the pain. This devastation reached for miles. All these bodies, someone's loved ones, all stretched out in death. Who would identify them? Who would tell their families that they had died, that they were so cruelly killed? Who would tell them that planes came and, without consideration, gunfire killed them? Why? These were women, old men, little children, and the disabled. Why? What did they ever do to deserve such genocide? They were not a threat to anyone. They were all just looking for safety–hoping to get away from the bombing–just like Wanda and her family.

The walk continued. As night approached, they looked for a safe place to rest. No shelter was available so they walked till they had distanced themselves from the horror. Exhausted, they bedded down in the ruts of a sugar beet field. The adults lay down again on the ground with a few beet tops for a mattress. The children were kept from the dampness by sleeping on top of the adults. Bernard unpacked the blankets from his bicycle and placed them over the children. In this way, they slept through the night.

As the sun rose, the family also rose and prepared to continue their journey. The sooner they got back, the sooner they could start living their lives again and get back to "normal." The hope of what was ahead urged them forward. Bernard led the way pushing his bicycle, while the women and children followed behind. As always, progress was slow with two tired little boys trying to keep up. If the walk was hard now, it was about to get worse.

As they went around a curve, a long line of Polish prisoners of war approached, guarded by armed soldiers. Bernard looked for a place to hide. There was none. He pulled his hat over his eyes and started to limp profusely, exaggerating every move.

The armed soldiers marched closer and closer. All the travelers froze and stared. A soldier approached Bernard, pointing a rifle directly at him, and ordered, "Drop your bicycle and get in line!"

Bernard spoke fluent German. The family had learned the language during World War I. He responded in German, hoping to gain some sympathy.

"But I need my bicycle to steady me. Besides, why do you want me? I'm old and sick."

"All men are supposed to help the Reich. You are no exception. Get in line!"

Bicycle in tow, Bernard limped his way to the edge of the procession. No hugs or kisses, no good-byes, no conversation with his family. With the bayonet pointing at his face, he had no choice but to obey. Leaving his family standing on the road, he went, separated again from those he loved. First it was his wife and child, now his mother, his sisters, and the little ones. What could he do? What choices did he have? As numbness settled over his body, he glanced at his family and joined the march. Perhaps they would meet again, somewhere, sometime. "Oh, Lord, let it be."

Meanwhile, the rest of the family mixed into the crowds of women and children and tried to continue on. How could they lose Bernard? Hadn't they suffered enough?

"Dear God, please keep him safe. Please, dear God, help us too!" Wanda prayed.

It would have been so easy to crumple up into a heap and weep. But they had to keep going. The children needed them. They had to keep them alive. Trying to hold back tears, they walked like robots, not even feeling their bodies, one foot in front of the other. Would they ever see Bernard again? Only God knew.

The rest of the journey was even more difficult. Without Bernard to help transport the children, the women had to take turns holding on to the three children. Many of the necessities were still tied to the bicycle. There was no choice but to go on and manage with what they had.

The next night was almost intolerable. Again, they slept in the ruts of a field. This time, however, there were no blankets to cover the children. Sleep did not come easily. Memories of the terrors of that day whirled around in Wanda's head. To calm herself, she went in prayer to her friend, Jesus. She prayed through the night for Bernard and for all of her family, until she dozed into a fitful sleep.

Chapter 10

Empty Pots

The unfailing love of the Lord never ends! By his mercies we have been kept from complete destruction. Great is his faithfulness: his mercies begin afresh each day.

—Lamentations 3:22–23

The journey continued back to Lublin, the largest city in southeastern Poland and not very far from the Soviet Union. The Nazis had just devastated this city, the intellectual center of Poland. German units with more than two thousand tanks and one thousand planes had broken through the Polish defenses. Hitler had not concerned himself with Soviet retaliation. He had just signed a non-aggression pact with the Soviet Union the previous month. The agreement was that Poland would be divided between the two powers.

Although it was just the third day of the return trip, it felt as if they had been gone for months. Sleeping on the ground, walking such long distances, and seeing such atrocities while lugging children and packages, had drained their physical and emotional strength. The food the Plitczeks had packed for the trip was almost gone. There was nothing to buy. Hunger and thirst were their constant companions. None of the women wanted to admit that they were hungry or thirsty. They were saving the clean water and the little food that was left for the children.

All day long they walked, even into the night. They were now very close to Lublin and did not want to spend another night sleeping in the fields. With exhausted bodies, they pushed on. Slowly, they pressed toward their goal. Through the great swaths of farmland that stretched as far as the eye could see, they walked. Down stretches of roads lined with trees and past the forested land that had sheltered them, they walked.

In the moonlight they could see the outline of the city. Would their apartment building still be standing? Had it been destroyed since they left? Did their rooms still have walls and ceilings? Was anything left? Was everything ransacked? What would greet them?

Wanda prayed as she walked. "Dear Jesus, I hope you chose to preserve our home. You know how tired we are. Please give us strength to continue. Only You know how we feel. You have been with us through all these unbelievable days. You saw us and sent Your angels. Thank You. Please watch over us tonight and help us."

As they approached the town, Danek started to cry. First softly, then he quickly crescendoed into a soulful wail. His wailing echoed across the fields and into the city. He would not be comforted. His two-year-old frame had endured more than he could handle. Tears flowed from his curly eyelash framed eyes and down his chubby cheeks. Wanda held him tightly and tried to muffle his cry.

From the edge of town, armed Nazi soldiers ran toward the women. A curfew was in effect and no one was to be outside.

"Who are you and what are you doing?" a soldier barked.

In German, Wanda replied, "We're just returning home. We've been gone for several days. We were told that we could return to our homes and live in safety."

Looking at the motley group, he asked, "Where do you live?"

"On Third of May Street."

Lowering his rifle, he said, "Go ahead, but don't let this happen again. Remember that there is a curfew and it is strictly enforced. You will be in great trouble if you do not abide by the rules. You will be questioned, imprisoned, or even shot. Remember!" he sternly said as he lifted his finger and pointed at the group.

Quickly, they slid away from the soldiers and walked toward their apartment. Among the destruction they walked, weaving through the many bomb craters till they reached their own neighborhood. Thankfully, their apartment was still there, just as they had left it the last time they were in Lublin. It was still locked and nothing had been touched. Quickly, they entered, had a little to eat and drink, and immediately went to sleep. Tomorrow would be another day. Tomorrow they would assess what to do next.

Morning dawned. Outside, armed soldiers supervised prisoners as they continued to clean up the city. Inside the apartment the family slept, grateful to again be sleeping on a bed with blankets and pillows. The noise outside did not disturb them. Everyone slept until mid-morning, when the children started to stir.

Fortunately, all the food that was stored up before the war started was still there. A large loaf of bread was still on the table; dry, but bread. In the pantry, fresh eggs were still in the large crock covered with a salt water solution. Potatoes, onions, and cabbage were stored under the table in a large box. There was rice, barley, *kasza* (buckwheat), and oatmeal. The homemade noodles that had been made with lots of eggs, dried, and stored in a pillowslip, were untouched. A large bottle of *smalec* (grease rendered from chicken fat) was ready to spread on bread or to fry some potatoes. Tea, wonderful tea, was still in the pantry and, wonder of wonders, coffee and dried milk accompanied the sugar and spices.

What bounty, what amazing, wonderful bounty! This food would last for quite some time. How thankful they were that God had saved their supplies.

A fire was made in the wood-burning cook stove. Breakfast was made, a soup made by boiling water, adding dry milk, seasoning it with salt, and then thickening it slightly with flour. It was served in large, white, enamel-covered tin bowls with blue rims. What a wonderful, wonderful, warm breakfast.

Today, the traumatized family just wanted to rest and be together. No one wanted to venture out. And so it was for several days.

Days passed, then, miraculously, God answered a prayer. On the doorstep stood Bernard. He was almost unrecognizable. His clothing was covered with ground-in dirt and his hunched over, exhausted body could barely stand. He hadn't eaten in days and hadn't found anything to drink.

He fell into the house and into the waiting arms of his mother and sisters.

After a time of weeping, he sat at the table and with trembling hands accepted the tin cup of warm milk. Even though he was starving, he could hardly eat the warm potato soup that followed. His stomach had shrunk and could hardly contain the food. It was time for him to rest. Everyone gathered around his bed while Anna stroked her son's tired, furrowed brow. In a soft slow voice he started to reveal how he had escaped from the Nazis.

"As I marched with the prisoners, I slowly started conversations with the Nazi soldiers. Little by little I talked my way into their graces. Because I spoke German, the soldiers did not watch me as closely as the others. As we walked down the highway, I slowed my pace. Step by step I edged my way to the end of the line." He closed his eyes and continued. "At an opportune time, I slid into the woods and hid. They did not miss me and went on without me." His voice slowed even more and got even quieter as he finished. "From there I went in a roundabout way through the back roads and woods. I was so tired. I couldn't push the bicycle anymore. I left it in the woods."

Opening his eyes he said, "Thank God that *you* made it here safely. Thank God that I am here. God is good!" His voice trailed off and he immediately fell into a deep sleep.

Bernard stayed to recuperate and rest for about a week, then he left to look for his wife and child.

Life in Lublin was very difficult during the Nazi occupation. Hitler allegedly said to his commanders, "I have issued this command: I'll have anybody who utters but one word of criticism executed by a firing squad. Our aim is to physically destroy the enemy. You are ordered to mercilessly and without compassion send to death men, women, and children of Polish race and language." This was done in order to gain living space (*lebensraum*) that they felt they needed for the Arian race.

Very little food could be bought inside the city. On the outskirts, soldiers prevented food from entering. Farmwomen would walk for miles to come and sell their wares. The soldiers would confiscate and destroy their wares or keep the products for themselves. The heavy cans of milk were poured into the streets.

Even though Wanda's family was very frugal, the food supply started to diminish. Because very little work was available, wit and imagination had to be used to earn some *złoty* (money).

Through a friend, Wanda heard of an opportunity to buy a large quantity of sugar at a bargain. She hired a horse and wagon and, at great risk, went outside of town to buy the sugar. She returned to town by a roundabout way, hoping the soldiers would not take her prize. At home, she immediately hid the sacks of sugar under the table, covered by a long tablecloth. Little by little, she sold the sugar by the kilo. The sugar was not for the family's use, but to sell.

"I can't seem to find my scissors," Wanda lamented one day. "I've looked everywhere and can't seem to find them."

Days later she found them, but only after finding her two little rascals sitting under the table, looking very guilty. Romek had taken the scissors, cut a hole in the sack, and hid the crime tool in the sugar. With a spoon he scooped the sweetness into a cup and invited his little brother to join in the misdeed. Both hid under the table and very quietly feasted on the sugar.

Another way to earn money was to sell cabbages. Again, Wanda hired the horse and wagon and with the driver went to a farmer to buy a wagon full of cabbages. The soldiers didn't seem to mind if cabbages came into town. They were unloaded onto the street. There she stood all day till every one was sold.

One day Wanda was selling cabbages at a farmer's market. A farmer came by with a wagon full of cabbages. Noticing that Wanda had just a small amount of produce, he said, "Do you want these cabbages? I'll sell them to you very cheap. I'm done for the day and would rather not take them home." She thankfully accepted and paid him. While she was arranging the cabbages on the pavement, soldiers came by in a jeep and taunted her.

"Hey, pretty lady! We'll take you for a ride! Get in the jeep."

"No, thank you. I'm busy," she retorted.

Continuing, they said, "Such pretty legs shouldn't be wasted. Come on. We'll have some fun." Then angrily, they said, "Get in the jeep!"

As they started to get out of the jeep, Wanda got scared and ran with the soldiers in pursuit. She was quick and knew the town. Running between houses and apartments, she hid in a dark arch of a walkway. Trembling, she pleaded, "Dear Lord, save me from these men. Save me for my children. Please help me."

A door opened in the dark walkway. A woman pulled her inside just before the soldiers saw where she went. Wanda hid. The soldiers looked in all the dark nooks of the walkway but could not find her, then left. Her cabbages stayed on the street and she never returned for them.

Another way they earned money was to make cabbage soup. Every night, a large amount of soup was cooked using fried onions, potatoes, and cut-up cabbage. The soup was quite tasty and sold well. During the day, Zosia and Wanda would stand on the street with their pot of warm soup and sell it by the cup.

Each day it became more difficult to feed the family. Many days each family member could only have one slice of bread a day. It was frightening. There was nothing to eat. Even the little boys noticed that there was no food.

One day, little Danek lifted the cover from a cooking pot and said, "Mama, does God know that our pot is empty?"

"Yes, dear, He knows," Wanda replied. "He will give us what we need."

This two-and-a-half-year-old child would often initiate Bible reading. He would take the book, open it, and say, "Here, Mama, read." Many times the text was exactly what they needed to hear, comforting words from God, promising that He would supply all their needs.

Miles away, Sabina, an old friend, lived on a farm. She had a strong feeling, as if directed by God, that Wanda's family needed food. She pondered the thought, but it would not leave her.

She took a large piece of linen, laid it on the floor, and put food in the center of it. There was flour, butter, bread, and cheese. On the very top of the package she packed up some fresh eggs. Taking the opposite corners of the cloth, she tied them together into a neat bundle. The remaining corners she took in her hands, swung the bundle over her shoulders, and tied the ends under her chin. With one hand under her chin she supported the package. With her other hand she held a container of milk.

This dear, godly woman walked five kilometers to bring her gifts to this family. Though it was very dangerous, she was compelled to go. As she approached Lublin, shelling started. Before she could look for shelter, a shell hit the ground very near to her. The impact was so severe that it threw her to the ground. Debris completely covered her. As she got up, she discovered that the impact had turned her around and thrown her exactly in the opposite direction of her destination. Fortunately, she was not hurt. After she recovered, she continued walking into the city. The soldiers did not stop her.

She arrived at her destination shaken and exhausted, but grateful to still be alive. When her bundle was unwrapped, to everyone's amazement, everything was in tact. By a miracle, not even one egg was broken or even cracked, and not one single drop of milk was spilled.

Did God know that the cooking pots were empty? Did He supply the family's need? Yes, a thousand times over! He knew!

Chapter 11

God Provides

"So I tell you, don't worry about everyday life—whether you have enough food to eat or clothes to wear.

"For life consists of far more than food and clothing. These things dominate the thoughts of most people, but your Father already knows your needs. He will give you all you need from day to day if you make the Kingdom of God your primary concern."

—Luke 12:22–23 and 30–31

As the friends sat at the table, visiting and sipping chamomile tea, they exchanged war experiences. Goose bumps danced on Wanda's skin as she recounted the many times she and her family had brushed with death. Why were none of them hurt or killed? Only God knew. He must have had a reason.

Soon the conversation turned to Sabina's daughter.

"How is your daughter?" Wanda asked.

"Not good, I'm afraid," Sabina replied. "Recently I heard from her. She was traveling north to a safer zone to stay with my sister. On the way, the whole train was hijacked by Russian soldiers and taken to Siberia. She wrote from Siberia and asked for warm clothing. Right now she is all right but I don't know what will become of her in that horrible, cold place. We have to keep praying."

The conversation flowed easily, as it does between good friends. Meanwhile, Czesia and Zosia busied themselves by preparing potato pancakes. Potatoes and an onion were grated by hand. An egg was added along with some flour, salt, and a tiny bit of baking soda. The batter was fried in *smalec* (grease rendered from chicken fat). The pancakes were served with a light sprinkling of sugar. This was truly a treat. For the hungry family, this was a feast made possible by Sabina, who listened to the prodding from God Himself. She walked through shelling to deliver the answer to a prayer.

The winter of 1939 was one of the coldest in history. The relentless subzero days continued without a break. No one went outside unless they had to. Even with layers of clothing, it was hard to keep warm inside the apartment. Though conserving coal, they knew it would not last the whole winter. Coal was rationed and could only be bought if one had a coupon. Wanda heard that some coal coupons would be available the following day at the town hall. She made a plan to leave very early in the morning to wait at the door before others arrived.

In spite of the curfew, at four in the morning she wove her way through the city. Dodging soldiers and shuffling through the deep snow, she arrived at the town hall. To her dismay, others were already lined up in front of the office inside the cold building. She stood in line for four hours before the office was opened. *This wait is worth it*, she thought. *Now my family will stay warm.*

The office opened and the line moved quickly. One by one, the people came out with satisfied looks on their faces. Now it was Wanda's turn. As she was about to step into the office, a clerk came to the door and closed it.

"I need to go inside. Please! I need a coal coupon," Wanda pleaded emphatically. "My children are cold."

"I'm sorry, lady. Everyone is cold. We have no more coupons." The clerk lowered his head and locked the door.

Dejected, Wanda slowly turned and walked back toward her apartment. Tears burned her cheeks as they fell and immediately froze to her skin. What could she do now? How would they keep warm and cook the food? How could she face her family with this disappointment? She did the only thing she knew to do. She prayed, "Dear Lord, I need coal to keep the children warm. You promised. You said that You would supply all our needs. I really need Your help. Please help me."

As she walked along the road, an old man pulling an empty horse-drawn wagon slowed down beside her and said, "Good morning, lady. Does lady need coal? I have an extra coupon that I don't need." She could not believe what she was hearing! Was she dreaming? Did she really hear what he said?

"What did you say?" she asked, looking intently at him.

"Do you need coal? I have an extra coupon," he repeated.

"Yes, yes!" Wanda said exuberantly. "I have three small children at home and the house is cold. I waited in line for four hours today, but when it was my turn, they were out of coupons."

"Do you need help getting the coal home? My wagon is empty and I can help you," he said.

"You are truly sent by God. Thank you. Thank you," she accepted gratefully.

That record-breaking cold winter the apartment was warm and helped shelter others who needed warmth.

At the start of the war, Lublin had 122,000 inhabitants, 37,000 of whom were Jewish. There were more than a hundred synagogues in the city. Lublin was the most important center of Jewish culture and scholarship in Europe.

After the war started, Lublin became the headquarters for the SS and the Gestapo for the administration of Operation Reinhard (the Nazi plan for "The Final Solution to the Jewish Question"). The headquarters for the Nazi party was also located in Lublin.

Two cities nearby, Zamosc and Tarnow, were the sites of Gestapo prisons. From there, the first political prisoners were taken to Auschwitz. A beautiful castle built in the 1820s, just east of the old town, was also used as a Gestapo prison.

At the beginning of the Nazi occupation, the Jews of Lublin were forced into ghettos. Some of the Jews were taken to a nearby cemetery and executed. Others were shot in the Krepicki forest. Many were sent to the nearby extermination centers. Eighteen thousand Jews from the Lublin area were shot in one day at the Majdanek concentration camp.

Most of the gathering of Jews was done at night. Many residents of Lublin did not know what was going on, or preferred not to know.

Little excuse was needed to arrest or shoot someone. Professional, cultured, and disabled people were taken away. The Polish culture was to be wiped out, along with the Jews. Unfortunately, no one could be trusted, not even friends or neighbors. Some would turn in false evidence in exchange for extra food or medical treatment.

Little comfort could be gained from husbands or sons. Most of the men were gone, fighting the war. Some were fighting with the Polish army, the Germans took some, and others were taken to fight in the Russian army. Wanda had no idea where her husband was, if he was well, or if he was even alive.

Communication with your loved ones was out of the question. No stamps could be bought and no mail delivered. Post offices were closed. Occasionally, a letter would be hand delivered through a friend or information was passed through the Polish underground.

In this environment Wanda's family tried to survive. Every day was a struggle. Each day, new ways had to be found for survival. Families of Polish soldiers were not compensated in any way. They all had to fend for themselves. When there was no money, they bartered. A scarf could be exchanged for a loaf of bread, farm work for some potatoes or produce, a little mending for some milk, and so on.

One day, Wanda came across a soap recipe. This recipe only had a list of ingredients, not the proportions. *I know I can figure this out and make some soap*, she thought.

For days she experimented. The kitchen stunk like a chemistry lab, but still no viable soap. "Daughter," Anna comforted, "you have really tried. It's all right. We'll manage another way."

Wanda would not give up. She experimented hundreds of times and kept records. Eventually, she came up with an excellent product.

Wood chips were boiled, strained, and added to the soap ingredients. This mixture was boiled until it became thick as molasses. She poured the mass into a pan and let it set. Later, she cut it into pieces and placed the bars of soap at the back of the stove to dry. She produced very nice beige bars of soap.

One day, the stove was very hot. By accident, the soap was toasted into a deep golden brown. She was horrified, but tried to sell it anyway. To her surprise, she found that it sold even better than the beige soap. From then on, she toasted every batch.

As an additional incentive to the buyer, she commissioned a local artist to whittle a mold for her. He whittled a beautiful elephant. With this mold she stamped the warm soap before placing it at the back of the stove.

Anna was an experienced salesperson. When her children were young, she owned a successful jewelry store. She volunteered to sell the soap. So now when Wanda made the soap, Anna went door to door and sold the golden brown elephant soap. Business was good. They could now buy a few of the necessities, but it was still very difficult to find them.

Once on a freezing winter day, Wanda set out to get fresh milk for her children. She had to walk a long way, all the way outside of the city limits. In the city, in pre-war days, all the ladies were expected to dress fashionably. They wore short dresses or skirts, nice coats, gloves, fashionable shoes, and perky little hats. On this day, Wanda dressed in the warmest clothing that she had. She had some rain boots, but did not have other appropriate clothing for this long trek in the cold. The exposure to the extreme cold caused her to become severely ill. An infection set in. Her head, ears, and throat hurt. Huge lumps appeared on the roof of her mouth. Her eyes were swollen, and she was almost delirious because of a high fever.

Where could she get help? The hospitals were not staffed. Polish doctors were taken as political prisoners. If any were left, they practiced medicine on the sly. Who could help her now?

God Provides

As a young woman, Anna had learned a little veterinary medicine. However, she cared for animals, not people. What could she do for her daughter? Wanda was burning up. Her fever was relentless. Even the little bit of aspirin that they had did not help.

First, Anna took towels, wet them, and wrapped Wanda's legs and arms. She placed another wet towel on her chest and another over her head. Several layers of heavy blankets were placed over her whole body. This treatment was repeated every half hour, but the fever continued. Wanda could hardly breathe. The pain inside her mouth and throat was so severe that she could not close her mouth.

Next, Anna turned Wanda over and performed an accepted medical procedure of the time. The skin on her back was exposed and she proceeded. Ten little glasses (like shot glasses) were lined up on the table. She poured a few drops of alcohol into each glass. In succession these glasses were lit with a match and immediately turned over and placed on Wanda's back. The fire went out, causing a vacuum action in the glass. The flesh was sucked into the glass. This was repeated till all the little glasses were lined up on her back. After about an hour, she removed them. They left little red circles all over her back. This procedure was meant to suck out the poison in her system.

Unfortunately, it did not help. Wanda's pain was unbearable and the fever did not break. She faded in and out of consciousness. Anna had done everything she knew.

Zosia and Czesia joined Anna in prayer, beseeching the Lord for His help.

"Our Father in heaven," Anna prayed, "we come to you as helpless little children. We've done everything we know to do to help Wanda. She's very sick and she is really hurting. We know that You see us and that You hear every word we say. Please show us how we can help her. Please help her to get better."

Anna continued with the compresses, while Zosia went searching for help.

Zosia occasionally did a little cooking for a lady with several children. This lady knew everyone in the neighborhood before the occupation. At any given moment, she could tell you exactly what was happening throughout the whole area. Perhaps she would know of someone who could help. Quickly, she ran to her house and shared their dilemma.

"Do you know of a doctor?" Zosia pleaded. "My sister is very sick. We don't know what to do."

Her friend paused for a moment then said, "All the doctors I know have been taken away. I know of a nurse who might be willing to help you. At least she was a nurse before the Nazis came. I don't think she wants anyone to know this."

"Can you ask her if she would come?" Zosia begged. "My sister has three small children and they need her."

"I'll try," her friend said. "If she agrees to help, I'll tell her to go to your house."

Zosia returned home, hoping that by some miracle Wanda would be a little better, but the fever continued and would not break.

It wasn't long before someone knocked at the door. Zosia carefully opened it. There stood a lady in her early forties. She was simply dressed, like a peasant. Her eyes were bright and intelligent. Quietly, she said, "Is someone sick in this house?"

"Please come in. Please come in," Zosia exclaimed as she practically pulled her inside. She took her to Wanda's bed and the nurse started to examine her. When she finished, she walked into the kitchen and talked to the three women. "I've seen this before, but never this severe. Without medicine there's not much we can do. I can lance the boils on the roof of her mouth...," then she quietly whispered, "but I don't think she has much of a chance. Perhaps you need to think about preparing a shroud."

The blood drained from Anna's face and she quickly sat down.

"Do you have a razor and some alcohol?" the nurse inquired.

Zosia found a straight razor that belonged to Wanda's husband. She opened the razor and ceremoniously sharpened it on a leather strap. When she was done, she handed it to the nurse along with the other things she needed. The nurse proceeded with the surgery. In just a few minutes, she was done. She cleaned Wanda's mouth and left.

During the war there were no funeral directors. Everything had to be done by the family. The family had to wash and dress the body and put it in the casket. Everything was done at home.

Anna was not ready to give up. She spoke with her daughters and they agreed. They would all fast and pray. Perhaps God in His kindness would answer their prayers and heal Wanda.

Chapter 12

I Cry to God

I cry to God without holding back. Oh, that God would listen to me! When I was in deep trouble, I searched for the Lord.

—Psalm 77:1–2

Anna continued hovering over Wanda. For hours, her daughter lay motionless. Then she would moan from the pain. All night long, Anna sat beside her child and prayed. She washed Wanda's lips with chamomile tea and continued with the compresses. By morning, Wanda was able to take a few sips of tea. Slowly, very slowly, she improved. The fever broke and she started to heal.

Over a period of weeks, Wanda continued to gain strength. God, in his mercy, allowed her to survive and regain her health.

As she improved, her vim and vigor returned. Soon it was impossible to keep her down. She was a strong-willed, energetic person and was the one who always made the decisions. Someone had to take charge. She did—and no one objected. Since the war had started, she was like a detective. Many times she would stay awake, looking and listening for danger. At those times, even sleep could not conquer her. She fiercely wanted to protect her family. They depended on her. It would be difficult for them without her.

A year later, conditions in bombed-out Lublin continued to be grim. Food was hard to find and clean water was a luxury. With the lack of proper nutrition and sanitary conditions, hundreds were dying. Every morning, carts would come by to collect the dead.

"Ela, my little Ela, how can I help you? You won't eat, my child, and if you do, nothing stays with you," Wanda whispered as she rocked her sick child. "You are so thin, my precious one. I wish I knew what to do."

Eighteen-month-old Ela had been sick for a couple of weeks but there was no doctor to help. She could not tolerate food and had bloody diarrhea. She was very weak. Whichever way she was placed, that's how she stayed. She lay motionless and looked like a skeleton. She could not move, turn over, or even cry.

Wanda hunted all over the city for a doctor, but had no success. Her last hope was to take Ela to the hospital, which was now only a repository for those who were dying. Without doctors or medicine, what could the hospitals do?

The *felczer* (town nurse) was at the hospital. She examined Wanda's child and said, "I'm so sorry! Your child has dysentery. We have a huge epidemic in parts of the city. Leave her here. She will die very soon. It won't be long. Leave her here."

Wanda picked up her child, held her close to her chest, and wept. "If she is to die, then let her die at home. I don't want her to be alone. I want to be with her."

"Is there anything that I can do to help her?" Wanda pleaded.

"I don't think anything will help, but you can try cooking some rice, straining it, and adding a little Saharan sweetener to the water. See if she will take it," the nurse suggested. "You could also try giving her plain rice water enemas to ease the rectal bleeding."

Wanda did as she was instructed. She fed the rice water to Ela with a spoon. With a little pump, she gave her the rice water enemas. After three weeks, nothing had improved but, incredibly, Ela was still alive. She was just skin and bones and still had bloody stools, but she was alive.

Not wanting to show the depth of her pain, Wanda went to the basement to pray and cry. "Dear Jesus," she prayed, "this child hasn't lived yet. All she has seen is war and destruction. Please heal her and let her laugh and play. I promise to teach her about You and how You came to earth to save us all. I know You love her and I trust You to care for her. Your will be done, not mine, but help me to be strong."

The whole household was affected by Ela's illness. Wanda hardly left the house. Even the boys tiptoed around and prayed for their little sister. Anna, Czesia, Zosia, and Wanda fasted and prayed, petitioning God on behalf of Ela.

God saw fit to let this child live. Slowly, very slowly, she improved. For a long time she was very weak, but she did survive and after a time was able to laugh and play and grow again.

During the Nazi occupation, all children were required to learn German, taught by German teachers. Romek and Danek had to attend a German school. It was the law. When Ela was two and a half years old, she attended *Kindergarten* (nursery school). The memories would remain with her forever.

Upon arriving at the school, the first order of business was the inspection for lice. Even the smallest of children had to line up and wait for their turn. One by one, they went into a little room and had their heads checked. If a child had no lice, a reward was waiting for him or her. A big, round table in the main room was circled with white, round candy the size of a quarter. No one could touch it until he or she was through with the inspection and given permission. This candy was given only to the children if they had no lice.

The school was a pleasant place, a place to be with other children, a place to play and sing and laugh. The atmosphere was cheerful and the teachers were attentive. Ela didn't mind that they changed her name to the German version of her name: Eli.

After lunch, all the children took naps on green canvas cots. Each child was given a bright, cheerful pillow. Ela had a big, multicolored, round pillow with bright flowers. After her nap, it was difficult for her to give up this marvelous object. She looked forward to naps just so she could hold this colorful soft pillow.

At lunchtime, the children sat at child-high round tables. Each table could seat ten children. Ela was fascinated and pleased to be able to sit on such a small chair, just her size. She had never seen anything like that. Everyone sat quietly until the meal was served.

A teacher came around and filled each child's bowl with a soup. But what a soup! It was a horrible looking black soup made of black bread. It looked like mud and smelled even worse. Ela looked at it, but to her it did not look like something you should eat. She pulled back and turned her face away from the soup.

"Eli, eat it all up!" the teacher said. Ela just looked at it.

"Eat it, I said!" the teacher raised her voice in anger. Ela did not eat and the children stared.

"Eli, did you hear what I said?" she fumed as her pitch got higher. Ela still could not bring herself to eat it.

Pulling Ela out of her chair, the teacher spanked her. Immediately, all the children started to eat the horrible black soup—all except Ela. She had to stand in her place at the child-sized table. The teacher stood close by, glaring. Tears poured down Ela's cheeks. She was embarrassed and tried to hide her tears by pushing both fists into her eyes. But the tears still trickled down from under her fists.

Things got worse! She was so upset that she wet her pants. A nurse came and changed her clothes. She dressed her in a special uniform used for such occasions.

To Ela, it was a wonderful outfit. It was a sun suit made of blue-and-white-checked material. Her favorite color was blue. Ela loved it.

What happened next, she did not love. The teacher found a tall stool and lifted Ela onto it. All the children gathered around her as she stood on the stool, and shamed her. "Etch-etch," they chanted as they stroked their pointer fingers together. They kept repeating this while Ela cried.

Children don't hold grudges very long. Ela was glad to be home and glad to show off her beautiful new outfit. Wanda washed the outfit and folded it neatly. Ela grabbed hold of it and wouldn't let go.

"This doesn't belong to us. We have to return it," Wanda said as she gently took it from her child.

"Make one for me, Mama?" Ela pleaded.

Ela had seen how her mother could cut up old clothing and make something for her brothers or for someone else. Wanda could take a discarded man's suit and make two little suits for her sons. She didn't use a pattern, just snip, snip, snip and it was done.

"Right now I can't. I don't have any material. When your Daddy comes back home, things will be different. I'll buy some pretty material and make some beautiful clothes just for you. You'll see!" Wanda promised.

As she spoke, she couldn't help but remember how it was when Józef was at home. She remembered many things, but started to reminisce about how they had met.

At first, she only saw him once, at a church meeting. It was hard not to be attracted to such a handsome man. He was a tall, strong, young man, with square jaws and dark, curly hair. He was a Christian. That meant more to her than his looks or his background or anything else. He asked for her address and they corresponded for many months, seeing each other only occasionally. In his letters he did reveal a little of his background.

As a child, his life was difficult. His father was in America hoping to earn an "impressive" amount of money so he could come back to Poland and build a house. During the time he was gone, he did not send money home to his family, so his dear mother had to work to exhaustion by taking in laundry and doing it by hand. Supporting four growing children was not an easy task. Having energy to spend time with them was even more difficult. The children missed their father and the closeness for which all children long.

When the Great Depression came, Józefs' father lost most of his savings. Upon his return to Poland, all he could buy was a cow.

At twenty, Józef went to another village to look for a better paying job. He lived with an uncle who treated him just like a son. This uncle fed him, helped him find a new job, taught him many things, and taught him new ways to think.

When Józef went back home for a visit, he wanted to share the new things he had learned. When he told his father that he had changed his church affiliation, his father became very angry.

"How could you leave the church of your childhood?" he screamed. He got so angry that he picked up an ax and chased Józef away from his home. Józef never spoke to his father again.

Wanda felt sorry for him and wished she could make it all better. Eventually, in a letter, Józef proposed and Wanda happily accepted. They had a beautiful but simple wedding and lived a good life together until World War II broke out.

Ela was only five months old when he left. Now she was almost three. She did not remember him or his touch or the way he used to gently stroke her cheek. For her, there had never been a male role model in the household. Józef had not been there to protect her, to care for her, to play with her.

Danek was two and Romek only four when they last saw him. What could they remember about him if he did come home? Would Józef be surprised to see that Romek, at seven years old, looked exactly like him and that Danek was a sweet, fair-haired five year old? What would he think? What would he say?

Wanda prayed for him continually. She prayed even though she did not know if he was still living. So many people had died. She had seen so much horror, so much death. It was her mission to continue praying for him. Perhaps God would spare Józef and bring him back alive.

"Wanda, Mama, Czesia, come here!" Zosia shouted as she came bounding into the house. Zosia's excitement brought Wanda back to reality.

"I have some good news!" she bubbled.

"Today I got a new job! I was cleaning in the village hall and an officer came by. I think the sun must have been shining just right on my hair. He watched me work and then smiled. He asked me if I would like a job working in his household."

"What did you say?" Anna questioned.

"Of course, I said yes! I'll be cooking and cleaning. It will be warm inside the house and he said he would pay me. His wife is expecting a baby and she has to stay in bed."

"How can you?" Wanda said in disgust.

"Are you sure you want to work for a Nazi?" Anna queried.

"I have to take a chance. We need the money. Don't worry. I have a good feeling. God will be with me," Zosia replied.

Zosia worked for the officer for many months. She was a good employee and even was there when the child was born. She felt comfortable and at home with the family and they with her. Eventually she got up enough courage to ask for a favor.

"My sister's husband has been missing for the past two and a half years," Zosia said. "She has three young children. Is there any way we could find out if he is still alive?"

The officer thought for a minute, and then replied, "Give me some information and I'll see what I can do."

Ela, Danek and Romek in Lublin after Ela recovered from her illness.

Chapter 13

Circle of Joy

There is a time for everything, a season for every activity under heaven. A time to cry and a time to laugh. A time to grieve and a time to dance.

—Ecclesiastes 3:1 and 4

"Zosia, come here," her employer demanded. Zosia wondered if she had done something wrong.

"I have some news for you." He paused. "Tell your sister that Józef is alive."

Zosia cupped her hands over her mouth as her eyes glazed over with tears. "Is he all right? Where is he?" she pleaded.

"He is all right and I know where he is." He paused again. "Would you like him to come home?" he asked.

"Of course! Of course! My sister will be so unbelievably excited. This is unbelievable! I don't know what to say." Her words tumbled over each other as they sputtered out of her mouth.

"I know where he is and someone over there owes me a favor. I've been wondering how to collect this favor. Now I know. Leave it up to me," he said, tapping his foot and nodding his head.

Within a few weeks, Józef returned home with German documents, allowing him to move about freely.

What an incredible reunion! Everyone was happy! Everyone was excited! The children jumped up and down because they were told that this man was *Tata* (Daddy). Three-year-old Ela did not remember him. Five-year-old Danek did not remember him. Romek, at seven, remembered very little of his father, but they were all happy, mimicking the behavior of the adults.

When the children were tucked away and asleep, Józef shared a little of his experiences with Wanda–but only a little. Wanda could see the pain on his face as he started:

"Our unit was in the woods digging trenches. The war had hardly started and immediately the Nazis took us prisoners.

"Conditions in the prison camp were terrible, monstrous! I wouldn't treat an animal the way we were treated. It was so bad that I can't even describe it. There was no food and we slept in the mud. People brought bread and handed it to us through the fence. If it weren't for them, we would have starved.

"I tried to dig my way out with a comb, but I couldn't get very far. I thought I would die. After some months, they asked for volunteers to go and work on a farm. I thought that this would be the only way I could get out from behind the barbed wire, so I volunteered."

With anguish, Wanda listened for the next sentence.

"That's enough! Enough!" he said waving his hand.

It took time for the family to get re-acquainted and start to bond again. Trust comes slowly. To the children, Józef was just another man. Most of the men they had seen in the last few years were men they could not trust. It was time for Józef to take charge of the family. The decision was made to move and start over in a new place. With the help of Zosia's employer, Józef got a referral for an office job in Turek. Wanda, Józef, and the children moved away from bombed-out Lublin to start a new life. Anna, Zosia, and Czesia stayed behind.

Turek was a bustling town with a lot of activity. It didn't take long to settle into an apartment, new surroundings, and a new job. Józef found an apartment inside a courtyard surrounded by brick buildings of different sizes. Beneath one of the buildings a large arched entrance snaked itself under a two-story house. The surroundings had a picturesque, old world charm.

Although the apartment was small and narrow, it was comfortable. It contained a tiny kitchen, a bedroom, and an all-in-one utilitarian living room. In this room, a bed hugged the wall and directly across from it a small table stood under the white, wood-shuttered window. With the shutters closed, the sunlight filtered through in thin strips as Ela peacefully napped, and outside the buzz of the flies serenaded her dreams.

In the corner stood a tall stove that reached to the ceiling. It was covered with white tile and had a small opening for stoking the wood fire. In this room the children slept and ate their meals. On the bed, Wanda ironed the impeccably clean white shirts that Józef wore to work. It was home.

Józef spoke German so he was able to work for a German insurance agency selling fire, life, and property insurance. His courteous ways, charm, and good looks made him an excellent salesperson. His appearance was always immaculate. Even his nails were buffed.

While earning a good wage, at last he was able to provide for his family in a reasonable manner. Now there was enough money to buy food, clothing, and even some furniture. And wonder of wonders, there was even enough money for a few toys. Wanda bought the boys a toy castle with lead soldiers. For Ela she bought some dolls and a doll buggy.

What a difference this was from what they had before. Wanda's prize purchase was a beautiful tapestry rug to be hung on the wall, as was the fashion. Cheerful, beautiful sunflowers were scattered all over the rug. It made her smile every time she glanced at it.

One of the first things they did as a family was to go to a photographer to take a family photo. Józef wanted to have a record of his family, a record in case something else happened and in case they were separated again.

Wanda dressed the children in their new clothes, Ela in a sweet white dress and the boys in German *lederhosen,* (short pants with straps over the shoulders worn by German boys). They all appeared to fit into the accepted German profile.

"Every one hold still," the photographer instructed as he put his head under a cloth and adjusted the shutter. Next he took a long pole with a trough on top. In this trough he sprinkled a white powder. Pushing the button on his camera, the trough exploded into a bright flash, filling the room with imitation sunlight. In a few days, the photo was ready.

"You know, Wandzia," Józef shared one day, "one of my friends at work told me about a sixteen-year-old girl named Basia. She needs work right away. We could hire her to take care of our children."

"Why? I take care of the children!" Wanda answered in an indignant tone.

"Well, her sister was just sent home from a work camp. Against her will, they gave her pills to stop her menstruation. She is very sick and has been sent home to die," Józef explained. "If Basia does not have work, they will take her to replace her sister."

"Oh, that's terrible!" Wanda said. "Of course we have to help. But what can I do while she is caring for our children? She has to have a real job or else the authorities will be suspicious."

"You will have to go out and sell books door to door," Józef stated.

"But Józio, I told you how I suffer if I go out into the cold. I never quite got over the terrible illness I had in Lublin. My head always hurts and I am prone to get infections." Wanda cried.

"I don't know if there's any other choice," Józef said. "That's the only job that is available."

That winter was intensely cold and it was difficult for Wanda to be out day after day selling books. She suffered with terrible head infections and many times had to take to her bed. In spite of that, she was glad that Basia was safe and had not been deported to a work camp.

Basia's father was a fine furniture craftsman. Although he was able to sell a few pieces, the family was very poor. At Józef's request he crafted a bureau and some additional furniture.

During that winter, Basia's eighteen-year-old sister died. With a broken heart, her father made a coffin. When he was finished, the coffin looked stark. There was no money for batting or material to sew a shroud. When Wanda heard of this, she immediately supplied yards and yards of lacy material that she had been saving to make curtains. With the lace, Wanda helped the women fashion a beautiful dress and a pillow. Enough material was left to elegantly upholster the inside of the coffin.

Gently, the family washed and dressed her body. As Wanda helped lift and put the dear girl in her coffin, a shiver ran down her spine. Jadzia's back was still warm. Just a few hours ago she had been alive. Now her presence was gone. Basia sobbed. Her mother sobbed. Wanda joined them. Jadzia looked so beautiful, quietly sleeping, just like an angel.

Basia stayed on and took care of the children. Winter turned into spring and spring into summer. The children loved Basia and enjoyed going to the park with her to play in the sandbox and just be ordinary children.

The family was together, the children were flourishing, and life settled into an acceptable pattern. There even was time for a little recreation.

Late in the summer, the family took an outing that they would never forget. The day was gorgeous! Józef took his camera and took lots of photos, but the memory of that day with the gentle breeze and fluffy white clouds would never be forgotten. It was a day they wanted to wrap their arms around and never let go. Among the many horror days of war, this was one perfect day, one special bright light.

Dressed in her red polka-dotted dress with the white pinafore, Ela ran along the edge of the wheat field. Her red bonnet twirled in her hand as she tried to keep up with her two older brothers.

Why was she so happy? Why was she so happy this day? She paused a moment, giggled, and then ran into the wheat field toward something red. No one stopped her. Her mother, father and brothers were there, all together. Today they were out for a weekend walk—all together. What joy, what contentment! Her joy was unbounded. No one prevented her from running freely. The warm breeze gently tousled her hair and colored her cheeks.

As she ran, the little red object got larger and larger. She stopped and separated the wheat with her hands. Ah! There it was—her trophy—a lovely red poppy. She plucked it greedily and searched for more. Deeper into the field she darted, stopping only for a moment to look to her parents for approval.

Oh the joy! They were all together at last. They were smiling and talking happily. Her spirit soared like the birds in the sky. She ran faster, in wide circles, laughing with glee. As she ran, she scattered the butterflies sunning on the flowers. The butterflies joined her in her dance of joy.

Again, she gazed around the wheat field. What were these? Pretty white daisies! Quickly, the white blossoms joined the happy poppy bouquet. She held them tightly, not wanting to lose even one precious flower. She ran and twirled and fell on purpose.

"Can you see me?" she giggled.

"Where am I? Come and find me?" she cried.

Soon, the whole family was chasing and dancing in the wheat, laughing and playing while the sun shone warmly on the happy circle of joy.

While further exploring the wheat field, she found a different flower. This time, beautiful, blue, puffy Bachelor Buttons enticed her. Wow! Was there ever a more glorious bouquet?

Her brothers, dressed in their *lederhosen*, joined in the hunt, but they were more interested in chasing each other than collecting flowers. Every now and then they stopped to pick a flower and ran to give it to their mother.

When the joy was almost too much to contain, it was time to go. Quickly, Ela picked a few more flowers and ran to her parents.

"Here, Mama, these are for you. Would you like some too, Tata?" she asked.

"Let Mama hold mine?" Tata offered.

"All right, let Mama hold them," Ela echoed.

Slipping one small hand into her mother's and the other into her father's strong hand, the circle was complete. This was her circle of joy.

Family portrait taken in Turek in case war split them up again.

Circle of Joy

Basia and the children playing in the park.
Basia's sister was sent home from a work camp in Siberia to die.
Józef and Wanda hired Basia so she would not have
to replace her sister at the Siberian work camp.

Romek, Danek and Ela standing in front
of the town cathedral in Turek.

Wanda and the children posing for Tata.
Wanda was a good seamstress.
She restyled used clothing into little suits and dresses for the children
and also made all her own clothing.

The children are happy. Tata is home.
Józef loved to take photos and
even learned how to develop them himself.

Danek, Ela, and Romek swinging in the park.

Ela with her doll after her father left for war again.

Chapter 14

A Time for Love

There is a time for everything, a season for every activity under heaven. A time to love and a time to hate. A time for war and a time for peace.

—Ecclesiastes 3:1 and 8

Life can change so quickly. Without a moment's notice, it can change. And so it was in early 1944. Józef was called to war and again had to leave immediately. This time, however, he had to join the German army. There was no choice. His new German papers (arranged for by Zosia's employer) showed him as being sympathetic to the German cause.

Again, he had to leave before arrangements could be made for the next step. What should Wanda do now? She wrote a letter to her mother and told her what had happened. Anna, Zosia, and Czesia had moved to Września several months earlier.

Their move happened this way: While employed in the German officer's household, Zosia did many things. One day she was sent on some errands. One stop was to a shoe repair shop. While there, she met a wonderful, gentle, kindhearted German cobbler. Her heart was immediately touched by his quiet compassion. She couldn't help herself. She fell in love.

Over the next few weeks, she took every opportunity she had to go to his shop.

It didn't take long for Leon to fall in love with Zosia. Soon, they were inseparable. When he proposed, without hesitation she accepted. A small wedding followed and they moved to Wrzesnia. Being the very kindhearted man that he was, he invited Anna and Czesia to come and live with them in their large apartment.

In the same spirit, Leon now invited Wanda and the three children to share the apartment. Wanda missed Józef but was happy to be reunited with her sisters and mother. How generous of Leon to let them come. He treated the children as if they were his own.

"I can't wait till they dry!" Danek said, pointing at the toys hanging on strings in the attic. Leon had cut out wooden toys and painted them in bright primary colors. *Pajace* are toy clowns or jumping jacks assembled with string. When the string is pulled, the legs and arms jump up and down.

"I'd like the one with the green hat. That hat looks just like mine," Romek announced.

Cross-legged, they both sat on the floor and watched the toys dry. Ela came and then the trio sat together, longing to touch the toys.

Winter was coming, so Leon busied himself and made wonderful felt winter boots for the whole family–no small task. Soon, seven pairs of green felt boots trimmed with brown leather were waiting for the cold and snow. These boots were the warmest, most beautiful boots they had ever owned.

The children loved Leon and took every opportunity to be with him. He spent time with them and cared for them and made sure they had what they needed.

In the spring of 1944 Leon and Zosia had a happy surprise: They discovered that they would become parents in the fall. As the child grew inside Zosia, they prepared the cradle and layette in anticipation of the birth.

Everything went well until late in September when it was time to deliver the child. The birth was difficult and the baby had to be taken by cesarean section. A beautiful, healthy little girl was born.

Two days after Jagoda was born, Leon came to the hospital dressed in a military uniform and accompanied by uniformed soldiers.

"Zosia, my precious one, I have to leave," he said caressing his wife and holding back tears. "I have to report to my unit immediately." The soldiers were there to ensure that he did.

"Let me hold her again," he said as he picked up his little child. Looking at the face of his beloved daughter, he could no longer hold back the tears. Tears streamed down his face as he caressed Jagoda and kissed her tenderly one more time. Whispering into her tiny ear, he placed the baby back into Zosia's arms.

The soldiers escorted him out and he was gone. Little did Zosia know that never would she see him again, that Jagoda would never feel her father's arms again and never hear his voice or feel his tender fatherly love. He was gone—gone forever.

The days passed and news was whispered about the horror that was occurring in Warsaw–the bombings, the death, the starvation, the total devastation and unspeakable atrocities. Wanda had many relatives and friends who lived in that area. Daily, the family talked and worried about them. Who was still alive? Who was starving? Who had died?

As the family kept talking and worrying, Wanda made a decision. "I'll go and find out who is still living. It's better to know than to keep worrying," Wanda said.

"Are you sure, Daughter?" Anna said with a worried look on her face. "I'm afraid for you."

"Don't worry, Mama, God will be with me," Wanda comforted.

"Then let me go with you," Anna offered.

"No, Mama, I need you to help with the children. Zosia has a child of her own now; she needs you. I know Czesia will help, but you know how much it takes to care for all these children. I'll take all the food I can carry and it will help them, even if it's for a little while," Wanda persisted.

They all helped prepare the suitcase. Dried bread and butter were the most important supplies. Butter was very hard to obtain so it was always a good barter item. The butter was melted and poured into bottles. Dried apples, prunes, and half a cooked duck were also added to the suitcase.

They looked around the apartment for anything they thought would help. Wanda found some silk stockings, pretty babushkas, and other good barter items. Last of all, she went to her linen closet and took out one last precious item–an orange. Oranges were very hard to get. When one was obtained, it was first placed in with the linens to scent them. Later, when it was time to eat it, it was sectioned and shared with the whole family. An orange would indeed bring a good return.

Wanda was ready to close the suitcase when Zosia said, "Wait, I have something else." She hurried to her dresser and pulled out a little white object. "Here, take this," she said. "Show them Jagoda's little undershirt. Tell them that among all this horror God gave us a new little life. That will cheer them and warm their hearts."

Wanda was ready. Her suitcase was full and a small satchel with personal items was flung on her back. She had just enough time to walk to the station before the train departed. But there was just one more thing to do before she walked out the door. As if by instinct, without saying a word, the family gathered in a circle, held each other and prayed, asking for God's protection, blessing, and guidance.

The train was filled to capacity, mostly with women and children. After an hour, the train came to a screeching stop. Everyone looked out the windows to see where they were and why they had stopped. Outside the train, armed soldiers stood waiting. An officer entered each car and loudly barked, "Open your suitcases, leave them on the seats and get off the train." Everyone did as they were told. They had learned this lesson many times before. You do not argue with a rifle.

Wanda stepped off the train and waited with the others as several soldiers entered the cars and came out with armloads of things they had looted. Other soldiers took their turn and did the same. When they were finished, they allowed all the passengers to get back onto the train. Wanda immediately went to her suitcase, expecting it to be disheveled. To her amazement, not one thing was touched. It was just the way she had left it. Not one item was missing. "Thank You, thank You Lord," she prayed.

The train continued. The scenery passed by the windows as the kilometers clicked away. The serene countryside changed into visions of destruction. Wanda closed her eyes and waited for the serene countryside to come back again. As they got closer to Warsaw, the train suddenly stopped again. "Why are we stopping now?" Wanda questioned the conductor.

"This is as far as we can go. The rest of the tracks are destroyed. You have to walk the last few kilometers," he responded.

With her suitcase in hand, Wanda joined the throng walking toward Warsaw. Little by little, the throng turned into a line as people got tired and stopped to rest. Wanda pushed on, wanting to reach Warsaw before dark. As she was walking, a jeep filled with soldiers stopped.

"Come on, young lady, we'll give you a ride," a soldier said. She hesitated—afraid to refuse and afraid to accept. She had heard of the atrocities that had occurred in Warsaw and was hoping that she would not be the recipient of the next one. "Get in!" he insisted. She felt she had no choice. Silently, she squeezed in between the soldiers, her suitcase perched on top of her lap. Her heart was racing wildly, like a pack of runaway horses. What did they have in mind? What were they going to do with her?

"Lord, what have I done?" she prayed in her distress. "How will I get out of here? Help me. Please help me, Lord!"

Before she knew it, her finger pointed to a house and she said, "I live there! I live there!" To her surprise, the jeep slowed down and they let her get out. She thanked them for the ride and, without turning her head, kept on walking until she was out of sight behind the house. There she stayed, till the soldiers were gone.

The remainder of the walk to Warsaw was uneventful, but long and tiring. When she reached Warsaw she was not prepared for what she saw. How does one prepare for viewing total devastation and destruction—destruction of the places where your loved ones once lived? Everything was destroyed. How could she find her relatives? Would she find them hurt? Had the soldiers taken them and tortured them? Had they died? Her thoughts ran rampant. *Oh, God, must I look at all this?* she thought.

It was getting dark. She had to find a place to spend the night. She climbed into a bombed-out building and found a concealed corner. She stayed there all night. Each time she heard voices, she trembled. She shuddered each time soldier's footsteps were in the vicinity. Sleep did not come easily, but she got through the night.

The next morning she started early, climbing over the ruins, looking for her family and friends. She asked if anyone had seen them. No one had. Landmarks could not be identified. All she could see was rubble, rubble, and more rubble. She searched among the ruins but it was hopeless. There was nothing to find. She saw people, all looking despondent. Any conversation she struck up produced more horror stories. She heard about the ghettos that were specially constructed for the Jews and how the Jews were starving. Their property had been confiscated, and they were forced to live like animals. They were tortured and killed by the thousands.

She heard the squeaky wheels of a cart scraping along the street. To her horror, corpses were stacked on top of the cart. She was told that every morning these carts came by. They were taken outside of Warsaw to be buried in a mass grave.

Wanda became very frightened. There was no hope there. Opening her suitcase, she shared some of her supplies with the children on the street and then rushed out of the city. Trying to look inconspicuous, she almost flew back to where the train had stopped. She felt defeated. She had not found any of her family and was coming back without any answers.

Chapter 15

Rescue Me

My God, rescue me from the power of the wicked, from the clutches of cruel oppressors.

—Psalm 71:4

The train ride back to Września was uneventful, although Wanda again had been changed. The new horror had been etched indelibly in her being. The countryside still passed by the window, the areas of destruction were still there, and life did go on but Wanda returned with sorrow in her heart. Perhaps sometime in her lifetime she would learn what happened to her family and friends–or perhaps not.

Life also continued back in Września. She had to get past this new horror that permeated her memory. After a while, she had to accept this continued display of death. *She had to! She had to!* This constant carnage could have her running, screaming through the streets. She had to pretend that it was common–an ordinary part of life–something that just happens every day.

Everyone in the family needed a diversion. The children especially needed cheering up. All this sadness was taking a toll on them too. Very rarely were birthdays celebrated during the war years but Wanda's birthday was coming up so the women started to prepare for a special treat. A birthday *tort* (a many-layered cake) could not be made on the spur of the moment. Ingredients had to be saved and gathered over a period of time. Sugar was rationed so it had to be saved until there was enough to make a cake. Butter was a luxury and also was saved and kept cold by placing it next to a drafty window. Flour came from the mill, eggs and milk from a local farmer. Dried apples, apricots, and prunes had to be cooked into jams.

The special tort recipe had to be mixed completely by hand. Czesia took charge of the batter and started to mix it in a big bowl. First she placed the butter and sugar in the bowl and mixed it until it was smooth and the sugar granules disappeared. Then she started adding the eggs, one at a time. There were lots of eggs. Next came the flour, milk, and the rest of the ingredients.

Czesia was strong and a hard worker. She could have mixed the batter all by herself, but because this was such a special cake, everyone wanted to help. The whole family stood around the table and watched as the ingredients turned into cake batter. Zosia, Wanda, and Anna all took a turn mixing the ingredients.

At last it was the children's turn. Romek was first because he was the oldest, then Danek, and then finally it was Ela's turn. Rarely did something like this happen. Cakes were something that only the rich had. They could not remember the last time they had had such a luxurious morsel.

The batter was now smooth and silky and a beautiful yellow. Everyone stood around the bowl and admired it. Even a few small fingers dipped into it just to make sure that it was good.

It was poured into round pans and taken to the bakery. The timing for the batter had to be just right because the cake was baked after the baker had finished baking the bread for the day. The cake was slipped into the hot oven and baked to perfection.

When it had cooled, it was cut into thin layers. Each layer was spread with a different flavor of jam. A frosting was spread over the top and sides.

The anticipation was almost too much for the three children. At last, the cake was done and it was time to lick the bowl and spoons. This was sugar heaven. Yum. Yum.

In other, better times, before the war, ice cream would have been ordered. It had to be ordered and specially made because the stores did not have freezers. It was picked up just before it was served and eaten immediately.

Everyone sat at the table and stared at the completed *tort*. At last, they could share the birthday treat. Ceremoniously they sang the traditional Polish birthday song, *Sto Lat*. They watched as Wanda carefully cut the cake. She served a slice to everyone and there was still half a cake left.

After thanking God for this special treat, everyone lingered over each bite as if memorizing the taste and wanting it to last forever.

"Tomorrow we will all have another piece," Wanda promised the children.

The birthday celebration was over. What a beautiful day it had been! It was getting late so the children were tucked into bed. *The memory of this special day will last for a long, long time,* Wanda thought. She sat in the quietness of the evening and mused over the day.

The loud rumble of a truck engine jarred her thoughts. *What is that?* she thought. *It sounds as if it's right in front of our apartment.*

Of course, being the curious one she had to immediately investigate. Opening the door she saw a large open bed truck parked directly in front of her building. Behind the steering wheel sat a German soldier.

"Why are you parked here? Who are you waiting for?" Wanda asked.

"We have orders to evacuate immediately. The Russians are coming!" the soldier replied.

"The Russians are coming? So why are you parked here?" Wanda questioned as fear gripped her heart. She remembered what she had heard. Some people said that the cruelty of Stalin even surpassed that of Hitler. He was killing thousands of his own people, by quota, without regard to status, position, or gender. He would tell his officers to dispose of so many thousands and didn't care if they were men, women, or children. He also had his own officers shot, at whim.

"However many soldiers come to the truck during the night," the German soldier continued, "I will take to the train. I have to leave at seven in the morning. The train will be waiting for us."

"Would you be willing to take us to the station too?" Wanda asked.

"If we have room, I will," the soldier replied as he rested his head against the back of the seat and closed his eyes.

Wanda dashed back into the house and excitedly announced, "The Russians are coming. We must evacuate immediately. A German truck is right outside our door. If he has room, he can take us to the station in the morning."

"Oh, no! Not again! Not more war and fighting," Zosia agonized.

"Haven't we had enough war? How can we live through more?" uttered Anna.

The instinct to survive was greater than despair. Quickly, the packing started. What should they take, what should they leave behind? Adrenaline flowed and packages seemed to emerge as if by magic. Only necessities were taken. Everything they took had to be carried. There was no room for toys or childish treasures. All of Ela's beautiful dolls were left behind. Romek and Danek's toy soldiers were left to guard the castle and other toys. Not one toy was packed.

Zosia packed everything that she needed for her four-month-old baby and laid out the *piezyna* (a long feather pillow used for babies) that would swaddle her child. The baby is placed at one end and the other end is folded over and tied in place. The little one stays warm and cozy inside her feather bed.

When the packing was through, there were twenty-seven items: nineteen packages and eight people. They took a sled to help carry the packages.

During the night, Wanda kept checking to see if there was still room on the truck. Not many soldiers had come. The truck still had room for them.

Before dawn, the children were awakened and dressed very warmly, one layer upon another. Everyone was ready.

Morning dawned, cold and dark. The sky was filled with giant snowflakes. It would have been a perfect day to stay inside and cozy up with a blanket. The snowstorm was so dense that only silhouettes could be seen. The truck was still in front of the apartment, but now filled with cold, wet snow.

Wanda and Czesia pushed the snow aside and loaded up the nineteen packages and the family. It was almost seven A.M. There was no protection from the snow and it was gathering on top of their heads and shoulders.

"Wait a minute," Wanda shouted to the driver as she dashed back into the house.

Quickly, she emerged carrying her beautiful sunflower carpet. She took the carpet and flung it over the whole entourage. This beautiful carpet, her prize, served as a protection from the heavy snow on the trip to the outskirts of town to the train station.

Everything was left behind; clothing, furniture, extra food, everything. No more thought was given to that special treat, the other half of the tort, which sat on the table, forgotten.

Chapter 16

Under His Wings

Those who live in the shelter of the Most High will find rest in the shadow of the Almighty. This I declare of the Lord: He alone is my refuge, my place of safety; he is my God, and I am trusting him. For he will rescue you from every trap and protect you from the fatal plague. He will shield you with his wings. He will shelter you with his feathers. His faithful promises are your armor and protection. Do not be afraid of the terrors of the night, nor fear the dangers of the day, nor dread the plague that stalks in darkness, nor the disaster that strikes at midday. Though a thousand fall at your side, though ten thousand are dying around you, these evils will not touch you.

—Psalm 91:1–7

The station was packed with soldiers and civilians, everyone hurrying and pushing, all trying to escape from the Russians. Although all could travel free of charge, the transport would be in a boxcar, not a comfortable, warm train.

Without hesitation, Wanda flung aside her beautiful sunflower carpet, which now was completely covered with snow, and left it on the truck. She left it lying there as if it were an ordinary rag, something absolutely worthless–just junk.

Nine-year-old Romek and seven-year-old Danek quickly jumped down from the truck and helped the adults with the packages and sled. Five-year-old Ela was lifted onto the deep snow covered ground while Zosia held on tightly to her precious little bundle, her baby girl. Anna and Czesia loaded packages onto the sled, but everything did not fit. Everyone had to carry something, even the children. They started to maneuver down the crowded platform, trudging through the snow, looking for space on the train.

Every car they passed was filled with soldiers. Where were the cars for civilians? They kept searching, pushing past the crowds, wondering if they would ever find a space.

Searching on another platform, at last they found the box-cars for non-military personnel. Again, they searched for an opening, a space large enough to accommodate all of them, but each car they passed was full. As hope was fading, they found an empty car near the front of the train, close to the steam engine. Quickly, they all climbed in and took possession of a portion of the straw-covered floor. Spaces in the walls let in the frosty winter air. After they had settled in, packages were unwrapped and more warm clothing was put on. Layer upon layer was put on in order to try to keep warm. Blankets were unwrapped and placed over the children and adults.

Immediately, others entered the car and it was quickly filled to capacity. The huge sliding door was pulled shut and before long, they were on their way.

This train was going west away from the advancing Russians, but there was no definite destination or scheduled stops. Some stops were short; some could last days. They traveled at the whim of the conductor, but no one complained. Everyone just wanted to go west—as far away as possible from the advancing Russian troops.

Zosia was still nursing her baby. She tried to keep her warm and fed but the anxiety of the ordeal dried up her milk. From among the bundles, she retrieved powdered milk, but where could she get some clean water? Her baby needed to eat. During a stop at a station, the steam engine hissed as they waited.

"Quick, give me a pot," she called.

She grabbed the pot and immediately ran to the front of the train, to the steam engine. Once there, she filled the container with the steaming hot water from the engine and ran back to the boxcar. The bitter cold air quickly cooled the water. Immediately, she mixed the powdered milk with the water and gave it to her baby.

The quick departure from Września did not allow for proper preparation for the trip. When most of the diapers were used, Zosia wondered what to do. There was nowhere to wash or dry them. How would she keep the baby dry and warm?

"Give the diaper to me, Daughter," Anna said as she took the icy, wet diaper and tucked it into her clothing, placing it against her bare chest to dry. As quickly as the baby was changed, the unwashed diapers were placed against the adults' warm bodies. There they stayed until they were dry and the baby needed them again.

Occasionally, food could be bought or bartered for, but not always. As time passed, the food disappeared. During that time the children could only have one slice of bread a day. Wanda chose not to eat anything and saved the bread for her children. They prayed and thanked God for that single slice and trusted that God would supply all their needs.

With the influx of people escaping from Stalin, the food supplies were strained. It was very difficult to find food, drink, or even clean water. Wanda and the children kept searching for something to eat or drink.

"Mama, why are you buying beer?" Romek questioned.

"I can't find anything else that's safe to drink," Wanda replied.

"I've never had beer before but I am very thirsty," Romek said.

"Sweetheart, I wish I could find something else, but there is nothing," Wanda replied.

The children and Wanda filled their arms with beer bottles and returned to the boxcar. The crowded boxcar was dark, cold, and foreboding. As night approached, the train started up again and the passengers inside fell asleep or sat quietly as the cars clacked over the steel tracks. Where would the next stop be? Would food be available there?

It was hard to stay asleep with all the people packed in so tightly, but what else was there to do? When the train finally did stop at a station, Wanda peered out of the door to see where they were. Dresden. Ah, Dresden. She was satisfied. The long row of boxcars stood motionless at the station of one of the most beautiful cities in the world. Dresden, the largest city in Germany, was known as a cultural city. Beautiful buildings, churches, arches, and exquisite statues were everywhere. Nazi soldiers joined the 650,000 residents as they came for rest and recuperation. They felt safe because this was one city that had not been touched by war.

On this day, Dresden was overflowing with refugees fleeing from the Russians as they advanced through Poland. Because the Nazis did not honor the No Aggression Treaty signed with Russia, the Russians were now advancing to conquer Germany.

All the refugees guarded their small spaces on this train, expecting that soon they would be moving again, going farther west, getting farther away from the Russian Army.

Wanda watched as her three children slept tucked in between the bundles of baggage. It was one o'clock in the morning and the train still stood in its place.

Zosia changed her precious little girl using another chest-dried diaper. She tried to nurse her but still couldn't. Instead, she gave her baby some steam engine water.

Anna slept, but only sporadically. Several times when Wanda woke, she heard her mother softly crying and praying.

Czesia slept soundly as she huddled close to her mother.

Everyone was glad to be on the train. But when would it move again? The night was progressing and the train was still standing as if glued to the rail. Time passed. More time passed.

Wanda, not known for being patient, stirred. Carefully, she climbed over people and baggage and moved to the edge of the boxcar. *Why isn't this train moving?* she thought. *I hear a steam engine idling, but where is it?* Through a hole in the door she peered out onto the other side. On the track directly across from their train, boxcars were lined up attached to a steam engine idling and sending clouds of steam into the night. She pulled open the heavy door just enough to look down the track. It looked as if that train was ready to go. On the side of a boxcar was a sign announcing the destination. *Annaberg? Oh,* berg *means mountains,* Wanda reasoned. *We could be safe in the mountains. We'll go to the mountains!*

Immediately, she sprang into action. Shaking her family awake, she said, "Come help me. We are going to the mountains." In a flash, the packages and family were out of the boxcar, on the ground, in the snow, and in the night. At the front of the idling freight train, the steam engine hissed and belched. Billowing clouds of smoke predicted the departure of this train. As they stood next to the boxcar, Wanda realized that all the huge sliding doors were shut. The doors were made of heavy wood and steel and stood high up off the ground. If they were going to board this train, they had to get on immediately. But how? Who would open the heavy door?

Without hesitation, Wanda hoisted her five-foot-two-inch frame up onto the Annaberg destined boxcar. Gritting her teeth and with supernatural strength, she pulled and pushed at the huge door. At first it wouldn't budge. With a few more tugs, the huge rusty door inched its way open.

Instantly, the packages, the sled, and the family were pushed through the opening onto the floor of the car. Never had anyone moved so quickly. Packages, feet, and arms flew everywhere. With her heart pounding and gasping for breath, Wanda stood on the floor of the car counting people and items: one, two, three, four, five, six, seven humans besides herself. Thank God, all the family was here. Now the packages: seventeen, eighteen, nineteen. What a miracle, everyone and everything was accounted for. As she pushed the door closed, the train started to move out of the station. The other train stayed behind.

Her family was alone in this huge boxcar. The car was empty except for piles of straw on the floor. Surrounded by their belongings, the women wondered why this train was empty. With all the crowding at the station, how was it that this train had no passengers? It seemed very strange.

Through the night and early morning hours on February 13, 1945, the train chugged along farther and farther away from Dresden, toward the mountains and Annaberg. They did not know that this train was going south. All refugees wanted to go farther west, away from the advancing Red Army, not south.

In the United States new technology had just been developed that allowed bombers to bomb targets at night. This was done to help with the war effort. Hitler had declared war on the United States and England and relentlessly wanted to conquer the whole world. The atrocities that he performed against the human race can *never* be justified. Millions of people had already died at his hand. This cruel, deranged tyrant had to be stopped. Hitler would not negotiate. Somehow the Allies had to get his attention.

During the night on the thirteenth of February, eight hundred Allied bombers arrived. Over two hundred more arrived in the morning. Throughout the night and into the next day,

Dresden was unmercifully bombed. The bombing caused a single inferno. The intense heat created a tornado like effect. Babies were sucked out of their mother's arms and flew in an arc directly into the inferno. The devastation was unspeakable. The whole city was destroyed. Between 35,000 and 100,000 people died. The city burned for days.

What about Wanda and her family? They were on a train going south, to Annaberg.

Chapter 17

Always Watching, Always Caring

I know how to live on almost nothing or with everything. I have learned the secret of living in every situation, whether it is with a full stomach or empty, with plenty or little. For I can do everything with the help of Christ who gives me the strength I need.

—Philippians: 4:12–13

At last they arrived in Annaberg, beautiful Annaberg. The sun was shining and the whole mountainside was covered with glistening white snow. Beautiful pine trees and deciduous trees lined the perimeter of the train station. A delicate breeze wafted across the branches, disturbing the snow and spilling it in cascades of diamond dust. Chalets dotted the mountainside and the whole area looked peaceful, as if one was walking in a snapshot of a beautiful vacation spot. It was magnificent.

Once out of the boxcar with bundles piled up around them, Wanda's family stood looking at God's beautiful landscape.

"Mama, I'm hungry," Danek said, looking up at his mother and forcing her back to reality. "Is there anything to eat?"

The children were hungry, always hungry. Everyone was hungry. "In a little while, I'll go and see if we can buy something," Wanda promised, hoping that this town would be different and that here she could buy some food.

As Wanda spoke, a delicious crunch was heard as someone bit into an apple. In unison, the children turned around. Close by, an older couple stood on the platform, eating apples. The children could almost taste the fruit as saliva flowed in their mouths. As if by magnetic force, the children were drawn to them. Standing directly in front of them, they stared. Like hungry little puppies, they could not take their eyes off the food. Wanda saw them, but did not stop them.

The couple turned to avoid eye contact. The children moved closer till they were standing in front of them again. The couple turned again. The children followed. Soon the pair felt very uncomfortable and started to squirm. "Children, would each of you like an apple?" the lady offered.

"Oh, yes, please," they replied without hesitation.

Receiving their prize, they thanked the couple and promptly returned to Wanda. Wanda watched as each child devoured the tasty treat till all that was left was the stem.

As they stood on the platform, breathing in the pristine air, Wanda silently prayed to her Heavenly Father. "Dear Lord, what now? Where shall we go? Please guide us, I pray. You've brought us to this beautiful place. Thank You. You always take care of us, but please show us where to go."

"Stay here while I go and see what I can find out," Wanda instructed.

In a few minutes she returned. "A wagon is waiting outside the station. It will take us to a resettlement area. There are many displaced people there, just like us." Quickly, all the baggage was gathered up and placed on the sled and they all trudged toward the horse-drawn wagon.

The bumpy wagon ride ended at a large building–a school. Inside the warm auditorium, people milled around, walking in and out of partitions made of sheets and blankets. The blankets were hung on wires and divided the hall into small family rooms. Families of women, children, and old men were housed together in that space.

The children helped Wanda, Anna, Czesia, and Zosia carry the bundles and sled into their very own compartment, their new home. There were no beds, no tables, just chairs. No one complained. This was a luxurious five-star hotel compared to the cold boxcar that had housed them for the past few days.

Their little space had an abundance of chairs. They tied them together to form beds, beds for everyone. Tonight they all would be warm and would sleep on chairs rather than among their bundles in the icy cold boxcar. That thought was incredibly comforting. The children could hardly wait to go to bed. Everyone started to relax, but what about food? They were all still hungry. Perhaps now they could buy some food and even warm it on a stove. It had been days since they had something warm to eat, something cooked on a stove. Hopes rang high.

"Mama, I smell something," Romek announced, sniffing the air.

"I do too. It smells like *zupa* (soup)," Ela added. Ela loved soup and always wanted her mother to cook some.

"Perhaps here we can buy something to eat. Let's go see," Zosia said as she took Ela by the hand. Wanda and the boys followed.

Someone had to stay in their little "room" to watch over the bundles. Leaving Jagoda in Anna and Czesia's care, they wandered down halls until they found the source of the wonderful smell.

What a sight! A dining area was filled with tables and chairs. The tables were lined with white soup bowls and big spoons. In the middle of each table was a huge plate of sliced, dark, whole grain bread. As the children stared, their eyes seemed to become as large as the soup bowls.

"Come and sit down," someone invited.

"How much must we pay?" Wanda asked.

"Just come and sit. You are our guests. Our townspeople have provided the food for you today. Just eat, there is plenty."

Food, warm food! What a blessing! How could they be so fortunate? They sat down, thanked God for this feast, and ate the delicious potato soup with *spatzels* (small dumplings). There was milk for the children and hot tea for the adults. No beer tonight. Today they actually had a drink that was appropriate for children.

When Zosia was through eating, she quickly took some warm milk back for Jagoda and told Anna and Czesia about their good fortune. Immediately, the two went to join the rest of the family, who were still at the table.

Bedtime came early on this day. The children were eager to try out their new beds. Wanda tucked them in and listened to their evening prayers.

"I'm going outside to see where we can buy food for tomorrow," Wanda announced.

"Czesia, would you like to come with me?" Czesia was always ready for a new adventure, although sometimes she hesitated because she did not want to leave her mother.

"Go ahead. Go with Wanda," Anna encouraged.

Together, they walked around the village and a little way up the mountain. On the side of the mountain, crowds of people stood gathered together, all looking in the same direction. Wanda wondered what they were staring at. The two sisters went to join the crowd. A shocking sight met their eyes. On the horizon, huge flames lit the evening sky. Black smoke billowed above the flames. It was frightening. What kind of a fire could that be? What was burning? People gathered together and stared in disbelief.

"That's Dresden burning. It was bombed last night and this morning," someone announced.

The fire burned viciously and lit up the evening sky. Watching the sight, Wanda was sickened. She had to leave. The sisters went back to the school and quietly shared what they had seen and heard. That night, the family knelt and thanked God for sparing them from death–again.

It was easy to settle in at the school. They now knew where to get the most important provision: food. There wasn't an abundance of food, but there was enough.

The hardest part of living in Annaberg was the air raids. The sirens would sound and everyone in the street would rush to a bunker. Those in the school would rush to the basement and wait on the prickly straw for the all-clear signal. Most of the alarms were false but could not be ignored. Anytime an alarm could signal another bombing.

"Mama, come here. Something is wrong with Danek. He won't wake up," Romek called to his mother one morning.

Wanda quickly looked at her son and immediately knew that there was a problem. Danek lay on his chair bed with his eyes slightly open, but not looking. His cheeks were blazing red. She felt his forehead. Danek had a fever unlike any she had felt before. He was burning up and barely conscious.

Immediately, she got towels and water and started the compresses. Hour after hour she sat beside her son and applied the wet towels. The fever was relentless. All night long she continued hovering over Danek and praying. Where could she get help for this child?

In the morning, Danek had not improved. He was still burning up and delirious. Wrapping him in blankets, Czesia helped Wanda put him on the sled. A doctor's house was on the other side of a huge hill, quite a distance from the school. Out in the cold, Czesia pushed the sled as Wanda pulled. On that snowy February day they transported Danek to the doctor as quickly as they could.

The doctor looked at Danek and immediately knew what was wrong. His tonsils were huge, almost choking him. He had a severe case of tonsillitis and a boil in his ear. The doctor lanced the boil and gave Wanda some aspirin.

"That's all I can do for him. I have no other medicine to give you. Take him home and keep him warm and quiet. The aspirin should bring his fever down and will help with the pain," the doctor instructed.

The sisters took him home and laid him back onto the chairs. Barely were they back when the drone of planes could be heard in the distance, followed by the screaming sirens. Immediately, everyone rushed to the shelters. Anna ran holding Ela by the hand, followed by Czesia with a suitcase and Zosia with Jagoda.

"Mama, aren't you coming?" Romek cried in distress when he saw that Wanda was not moving.

"Run, Romek! Run! I'll stay with Danek. He is too sick to move," Wanda yelled.

Romek obediently ran down the curved cement stairs to the basement and stood on the straw beside the rest of the family.

"Where are Wanda and Danek?" Anna anxiously asked.

"Mama is staying with Danek," Romek replied with a quivering voice. "She said that he is too sick to move."

The planes came closer and closer. Swarms of planes could be heard. Soon the noise was thunderous and the bombs started to drop. Wanda shuddered and shook but sat beside her sick son as the bombs exploded. She was scared, very scared, but kept focusing on the One who always gave her strength, the One who always watched over her.

God in His mercy protected the school and its residents and allowed Danek to recover.

There were many more air raids. As before, Wanda's family slept with their clothes on and had a suitcase packed with essentials. Many times the sirens would sound in the middle of the night. The whole family would run to the shelter in the basement and spend the night sleeping on the straw. The straw was prickly, but no one noticed, no one complained.

After a few weeks, the family was assigned to a more private area within the three-story building. An empty attic room would be their next home. The small room had one small window and was furnished only with a few chairs and a table. Straw covered the wood-planked floor and was used as padding under the blankets. These beds were more comfortable than sleeping on the chairs. They were thankful for the new accommodations. The children slept in the area where the floor meets the roof. Ela's "bed" was right under the roof. The ceiling beams were just above her chin. It was a cozy corner inviting the children to rest.

Several weeks had passed since they had arrived at the school. "I think these children have forgotten how to laugh," Anna said. "They are much too serious."

"They haven't had any reasons to laugh lately. What can we do to bring some joy into their lives?" Zosia asked.

Wanda and Zosia decided to put on a show. Not many props were available, but they used what they could find. The children sat cross-legged on the floor, waiting, anticipating. Something good was coming, but they didn't know what.

First, the sisters pushed aside all the straw and made a clear "stage" for their show. Then Wanda sat at the little table holding a newspaper, pretending to read. A plate holding pieces of pancake was set beside her. With her fork she stabbed at a piece of food and lifted it toward her mouth, then, pretending to be engrossed in the paper, she held the morsel up in the air. Zosia came from behind and grabbed the piece of food. The children laughed as Wanda pretended not to know what happened to the piece of food.

The show continued. The more the children laughed, the more ridiculous the show became. Zosia was a wonderful clown. She could kid around and didn't mind looking foolish. The show ended with a grand finale, but should have had a warning: "Do Not Try This Yourself!"

As Wanda continued to read, Zosia took a match and lit the corner of the newspaper. Of course, this was very exciting as they pretended to be scared and in a panic while they put out the fire. The children howled and could hardly contain themselves. For these children who had nothing, this entertainment was amazing, something they would never forget, and something they would remember the rest of their lives.

There were no toys, so anything that was found became a toy.

"What are you holding in your arms?" Wanda almost shrieked at Romek one day.

"I found it outside and thought I could have it," Romek replied.

Carefully, she took the item from his hands and ran down the stairs and outside.

She ran across the street to an empty field and carefully laid down a live artillery shell.

Back in the room, Romek was on the verge of tears. "What did I do wrong?" he asked with a quaking voice.

"You can't play with a shell! It's like a bomb!" Anna cautioned. "It could explode and hurt you. Don't ever touch one again or even go near one! Promise?"

"All right. I promise. But can I keep this?" Romek asked, his voice still trembling as he reached for a helmet.

"I think that would be all right," Anna replied as she gave him a hug.

Spring arrived and with it came the showers. It felt good to be out and about the town in the fresh air. The sound of horses' hooves as they pranced on the cobblestone street helped Wanda recall a happy time when she lived in Warsaw. She remembered how a *doroszka* (horse-drawn buggy) ran away with two horses. No one was making an effort to stop them ... so she did. She ran after the horses and grabbed the reins and hung on till the horses stopped. She had to smile at the memory. She had spent many happy hours around horses–magnificent horses.

Zosia enjoyed window-shopping. One day as she was browsing, it started to rain. She had no umbrella so started to run back to the school. Slipping on the wet cobblestones, she fell to the ground. As she tried to get up, her leg felt hot, as if it was on fire. It was impossible for her to get up, much less put any weight on it. People gathered around as she sat on the ground, her face twisted with pain.

"Are you all right?" someone asked.

"I don't think so. I can't move my leg," she cried. "Can you go and get my sister? She's at the school."

In a few minutes, Wanda was there just as a *doroszka* offered to take Zosia to the hospital. Without X-rays or doctors, the hospital staff did the best they knew how, but who knew if the leg was set correctly.

With a cast on her leg, Zosia returned to the school. No crutches or wheelchairs were available so Wanda carried her on her back. The cast stayed on for several weeks. During that time, there were many air raids. Each time, Wanda carried her to the shelter, on her back, like a sack of potatoes.

When the cast came off, Zosia limped. She continued limping even after the pain disappeared.

One beautiful spring morning, Wanda took her children into the mountains to buy some goat cheese. She had directions to a small cottage where she could buy the cheese. Cheese—what a treat! Everyone in the family loved cheese. Wanda led the way and the children followed like little mountain goats.

Arriving at the cottage, Wanda asked if she could buy some cheese. An elderly couple invited her in. As she entered the home, she stepped on the threshold. Immediately, the couple went into hysterics. The man screamed and cursed. The old lady held her head and rocked back and forth in distress. She even wept as if something tragic had just happen.

"You stepped on our threshold!" the old woman wailed. "Why did you do that? We offered to sell you some cheese and this is how you repay us? You have cursed us. Now our goats will go dry. We will have nothing to sell and we will starve."

Wanda felt awful! She didn't know that stepping on the threshold was forbidden. She did not know of their superstition. Quickly, she thought of a plan.

"Don't worry," she said. "Tomorrow, all four of us will return. As the sun rises we will come and take the curse off your goats and your house. We will have a special ceremony. You will see! Your goats will give lots of good milk. We'll be back at dawn. I promise!"

Wanda and the children walked back to the school. Their food supply was meager and she really needed to buy the cheese. They had bread and dried prunes, but cheese certainly would have made their meal taste like a banquet.

Early the next morning, Wanda dressed her children in outrageous costumes. They were a sight to behold! She had made costumes from borrowed items. Rags and ribbons hung from every part of their bodies. She made a head dress from "magic herbs" for herself and for each child. Sticks were stuck into the headdress so it looked like a crown. Borrowed cowbells and pot covers would accompany the "ceremony."

As the sun peeked out from over the mountain, the four arrived at the cottage. With the old couple watching, the ceremony started exactly as Wanda had promised. She told her children, "Just do everything I do."

Slowly they started dancing in a circle. They chanted made-up words as they gently banged the pot lids and rang the cowbells. With each turn of the circle, the tempo and noise got louder and louder. Soon, all four were yelling and screaming at the tops of their voices as they danced with passion.

The couple stood there mesmerized, as if witnessing a miracle. Were they truly believing that what Wanda and the children were doing was removing the curse?

Soon, with each step, the tempo got slower and their voices got softer. As the ceremony ended, they brushed the ground with their fingers and chanted their way toward the old couple. Finally, finishing with a flourish, they waved their fingertips over the threshold and in unison recited the "magic" words. The ceremony was over.

Extending her hands toward the family, the old lady smiled and, with tears in her eyes, profusely thanked them. Her husband was so pleased that he offered a whole wheel of cheese—the size of a dinner plate—free of charge. It was a wonderful, unexpected gift. It would provide many tasty meals for the family. Carefully, Wanda carried it back to the school.

The weeks and months flew by. In March, Ela turned six, Danek turned eight in April, and Romek was waiting for September when he would turn ten.

Many rumors were passed around and it was almost impossible to discern which ones were truthful. One day they woke to lots of commotion and excitement. People were running around saying, "The Russians are coming, the Russians are coming!"

"All the stores will be open this weekend. The storekeepers would rather give everything away than to have the Russians confiscate it. Quick, go buy! Everything must be sold and is very inexpensive," people excitedly informed.

For a moment, Wanda watched as everyone dashed around. All of a sudden, she saw women rushing up and down the stairs with food in their arms or in skirts pulled up to form containers.

"Where did you get that?" she asked.

"There's a secret room upstairs filled with food. They opened it and want everyone to take as much as they wish. They are giving it away free. They don't want the Russians to have it," a woman said as she rushed down the stairs.

Immediately, Wanda ran back to her family and said, "Hurry, everybody! Follow me. They're giving away food on the third floor. Let's go!" Anna, Czesia, and the children ran behind

Wanda. Even Zosia came with Jagoda in her arms. They followed the people to the mad scramble.

There, a storeroom was filled with food. It was *pełno* (full). It was awesome! Amazing! There were crates of sardines, huge wheels of cheese, sugar, powdered milk, flour, powdered eggs, cigarettes, and many other things.

Everybody was grabbing as much as they could carry. Danek snatched a carton of cigarettes. A man came along and said, "You're too young to smoke," and took it out of his hands and left without a second glance at the boy. Danek had taken the cigarettes knowing that this was a barter item that could buy bread. Quickly, he found another carton and hid it under his shirt.

Romek took a large case of sardines. Lugging it with all his might, he started back to the family's room. Stopping to rest, he placed it on the stairs. Another person came along and said, "That's too heavy for you. Go get your mama. I'll watch it for you." When he returned, the case was gone.

Back in the attic room, the family was thrilled with the abundance of food. Not knowing what tomorrow would bring, they ate their fill. "Eat, eat today!" Wanda always prodded. "Tomorrow you may not have anything."

What people were saying was the truth. The Russians did come. It was hard to look at them and not feel dread.

A few days later, in the town square, Russian and German soldiers arrived on motorcycles from opposite directions. They came and conducted a short ceremony acknowledging the end of the war. Everyone observed the stern faces, the salutes, the stiff marching. Announcements were made to inform the people that the war was over and it was now safe to return home. Transportation by train would be provided to everyone, free of charge. To end the ceremony, the two officers, Russian and German, shook hands.

Within a short time, the displaced people started to pack up and leave, returning to their origins. Zosia traded the sled for a buggy and prepared to leave Annaberg. Within a few days, the whole family joined the swarms of people returning home with hopes that home still existed.

Chapter 18

A New Oppressor

God is our refuge and strength, always ready to help in times of trouble.

"Be silent, and know that I am God! I will be honored by every nation. I will be honored throughout the world."

—Psalm 46:1 and 10

"Mama, where are you?" Ela softly cried as she sat obediently on the suitcase in the bombed-out train station. "I'm so scared! I can't see you!"

The early morning sun was rising on that cool morning in Dresden, Germany. From Annaberg the train stopped in Dresden. All passengers had to disembark and change trains. Wanda's family had to spend the night on the concrete platform and wait for the next train.

Wanda had been missing all night and Ela was terrified. She wanted to scream, but knew that she must not attract attention to herself. She muffled her cries but the tears wouldn't stop. Nearby, Romek and Danek huddled together beneath a blanket while Czesia held Jagoda tightly in her arms.

"Ela, sit on the suitcase and don't move," Anna had instructed her just before she left. *Where did Grandma Anna go and why isn't she back? Where is my mama? Where is Aunt Zosia?* she wondered. A few feet away from her, on her left, was a pile of straw. Protruding from the straw were two legs with shoes on. The legs belong to a man who was lying on his back–dead.

Ela knew he was dead. He didn't move or even twitch. No one was anywhere near him. Perhaps the gunfire last night killed him. Wanda always kept the children's eyes diverted from these kinds of sights, but where was she now? Why wasn't she there to tell Ela to turn away?

The night before, the train station had been filled with refugees. No trains were leaving and everyone was just waiting. When it got dark, people huddled in bunches and tried to reserve their spot on the platform. As the night progressed, they settled down to sleep on the cold concrete platform. With their bundles and packages surrounding them, they tried to stay warm and get through the night.

Wanda and her family did the same. As the cold damp air gathered around them, they tried to sleep. The night was quiet except for muffled voices, the cries of a few babies, and the rhythmic cadence of armed Russian soldiers.

During the night, a Russian soldier came marching in with a flashlight, flailing a handgun. He was drunk. Cursing and tripping across the platform, he flashed the light onto the faces of the people trying to sleep. With his handgun he poked around the blankets.

Trembling, Wanda pulled her babushka over her face and huddled closer to her children.

Pushing his way around the refugees, he groped through the blankets and tripped over legs. Closer and closer he came to where Wanda's family was sleeping. What was he looking for?

"Close your eyes. Pretend to sleep," she whispered to her children as she pulled the blanket even farther over their faces. Within moments, he was standing directly in front of them. Jerking back the blanket, he exposed Wanda's face. Smirking, he leaned back with satisfaction and said, "You! Come with me." He pointed his revolver directly at Wanda's face.

What could she do? Could she argue with a revolver? Trembling, she rose and walked away from her children and her family. She walked ahead of him to where he pointed. Through the long station they walked till they reached an office in a bombed-out building. Pushing the revolver into her back, he forced her into the room. With a large old-fashioned key, he locked the door.

Putting the revolver down on the desk, he started to undress. Wanda's heart pounded loudly within her chest and her mind spun as she tried to think of a way to escape. "I'm married and have three children," she blurted out. She quickly pulled a photo out of her pocket and showed it to him. Ignoring her photo, he retorted, "We are your liberators. We rescued you from the Nazis. You should give yourself to me willingly."

Quickly, she sent a silent prayer to heaven. *Lord!* she pleaded, *please help me! Please keep him away from me. Help me to escape.*

As the soldier undressed, her eyes hastily swept the room. The key was still in the locked door. While his trousers were around his knees, she raced to the door, turned the key, pushed opened the door, and ran. In and over the ruins she climbed. She ran deeper and deeper into the rubble until she found a hiding place in a corner of a bombed-out building. There she stayed, huddled in a ball, praying.

In the distance she could hear the man yelling, cursing, and shooting as he searched for her. Not finding her in the ruins, he returned to the platform. Again, with his revolver, he sifted through the blankets. When he could not find Wanda, he left.

All night long Wanda hid in the ruins, shivering. She didn't dare move from her hiding place. Fearing that the soldier was still in the area, she stayed very quiet, hardly daring to breathe.

Very early in the morning, when the sun was just rising, she heard a voice calling. She still didn't dare move. Again the voice called, "Wanda, where are you?" It sounded like her mother. The voice came closer, "Wanda, where are you? It's all right to come out." Very cautiously she climbed out of her hole. When she saw her mother, she ran into her arms and wept. Anna did not ask her any questions, she just held her tightly.

"Sit down for a moment," Anna said as she encouraged Wanda to sit and compose herself. "I have to tell you something. Zosia is missing. We have to find her."

Putting her head down into her hands, Wanda wept and prayed, "Oh no, Father, not her! Please help us find her."

Separating, they started looking for Zosia. Wanda went to the station while Anna continued looking in the ruins.

Still trembling, Wanda searched throughout the whole station. Fear still gripped her, fear that she would meet the soldier from the night before. Praying for courage, she continued. In and around and under the boxcars she searched. Not finding her, she climbed on top of the boxcars and looked as far as her eyes could focus. "Zosia, where are you?" she cried out desperately. "Zosia, can you hear me?" Not finding her, she continued searching through a line of empty boxcars.

As she looked deep inside one of the cars, she saw a figure huddled in a dark corner. "Zosia, is that you?" she called. No one answered. No one moved. Wanda looked again, then climbed into the boxcar. It was Zosia. Her sister stayed huddled in the corner, hugging her knees. Without speaking, Wanda sat down beside her and held her. Words were not needed. She had found her sister and that was enough.

"Let's go back to our family. Let's go back to Jagoda," Wanda coaxed. Together, they walked back. Anna was there, waiting.

When Ela saw Wanda, she ran to her mother, wrapped herself around her, and wept.

Chapter 19

Boxcar to Horror

Be strong and courageous! Do not be afraid of them! The Lord your God will go ahead of you. He will neither fail you nor forsake you.

—Deuteronomy 31:6

O Lord, rescue me from evil people. Preserve me from those who are violent, those who plot evil in their hearts, and stir up trouble all day long.

—Psalm 140:1–2

As the sun rose higher over the horizon, it warmed the station and the travelers waiting for passage back to their homes. Dresden was still in ruins. The devastation of February 14 had not been wiped away. Skeletons of buildings stood, reminders of what used to be. At the station, the roof hung in pieces with sky showing through. Boards were strewn everywhere and cavernous concrete holes were mixed with rubble and straw. Not all of the rail tracks were repaired.

Straw was everywhere. The station had piles of straw. People slept on it, covered up with it for warmth, died on it, and were hidden under it after death so that children would not have to look at the face of death.

Surrounding the station were buildings, also destroyed by bombs. Only pockets of houses were still inhabitable. Occasionally someone would weave his or her way through the rubble and disappear.

Months ago, before the bombing of Dresden, people were packed onto this platform like sardines. All were waiting for a train, hoping it would take them to safety. Those people were gone now. Most were not alive anymore. Today groups of people had gathered with their bundles, waiting for transportation *back* to their towns and villages. They needed to return to their homes, their families and friends. They needed to know who had survived and if it was possible to live in the places they left before they escaped.

Although the war had ended, danger lurked everywhere. Families were still afraid of being separated. Soldiers were still milling around with their rifles. Why? Why were bayonets attached to their rifles? Why were they still mistreating people? Why were they still using force, shooting, and killing?

Everyone wanted to leave this station as soon as possible. On this part of the return trip, a wooden boxcar would again be the transportation. When would it leave? Exactly where would it go? Only God knew.

Several families joined Wanda's family and together made preparations for the rest of the journey to Poland. All hoped to share the same boxcar. Waiting at the station, sharing the same fears and the same enemy, bonded strangers into a "family." A few older men were in that group. They took charge of the preparations.

An empty boxcar was found at the far end of the station. This car was shaped like a big brown box except for the top. On top, on the outside, a long covered trough protruded from the length of the car. It was used for blocks of ice when perishables were transported. The boxcar was dark except for a few rays of light that entered between the slats, and for now, through the huge, rusty, sliding door that was left wide open. Straw was piled inside the car. The opposite side of the car also had a sliding door but this door was wired shut from the inside. At the narrow end of the car, another smaller door was closed and wired shut.

The men went scavenging through the ruins to see what could be salvaged for the trip. A heavy, cast iron, wood burning stove was found. Three of the men lifted it and loaded it into the boxcar. A small hole was cut in the roof for the chimney and the stove was installed in the middle of the car. Scraps of wood were found and piled up inside. This wood was to be used for heating and cooking.

The only way to get safe drinking water was to boil whatever water was found or to "borrow" some from the valve of the huge black steam engine. A walk to the front of the train would, hopefully, satisfy that need. There, gratefully, the engineer would turn away as people helped themselves to the precious water.

Bathroom facilities would be just a tin bucket in the corner. Someone would hold up a blanket for privacy. This was emptied whenever the train would stop or, at an opportune moment, dumped out the back door while in transit.

No one knew exactly how long this trip would be. It could be days, weeks, or even longer. No one knew when this car would join a train, exactly where it was going, or what the scheduled stops would be. All they knew was that it was going east, to Poland. This was like embarking on a sea without a rudder or compass and not knowing where the wind would blow. Would they come to safety or be dashed against the rocks?

After the bundles of luggage, baby buggy, food, cooking utensils, and supplies were loaded, the travelers climbed in. Anna, Czesia, and Zosia holding Jagoda, joined Wanda and the children in the middle of the boxcar. They joined the other passengers and now the car was full.

Once inside, everyone felt safer. Wanda's family was together and for now was warm and cozy on the straw in their own little section of the car. Their spot was close to the front by the pot-bellied stove, to the left of the sliding door. This was their "home." They set about "decorating" it. The suitcases and bundles were placed at the head. Blankets were spread over the fluffed up straw for a common bed. Other blankets were used as covers.

As the evening light faded, the huge rusty doors were pushed shut and wired from the inside. All the anxious, wide-eyed people were now doomed to a destiny that no one could predict. Everyone hoped and prayed that this trip would take them home to safety, a place where one could live without bombs falling and rifles tearing through people and buildings. They hoped to be in a place where human beings were regarded with worth rather than just another target to show how powerful the rifle holder can be.

Wanda's children and Jagoda were the only children in the boxcar. Romek, Danek, and Ela immediately were taught a strict code of behavior that they must obey. It was of paramount importance that they be very, *very* quiet. If soldiers were nearby, they were not to make any, *any* noise. They were not to move or rustle the straw, and barely breathe. They had to be inconspicuous. They were not to call attention to themselves or the boxcar. Though bonded through circumstance, the traveling companions were concerned. Would it be safe to travel with children? Could they be trusted to keep the code of silence?

The men, dressed in ragged clothes, looked old and tired. With hope for a better future, the women were eager to leave and start a new life in familiar surroundings. Because they had spent days in the same clothing, and slept in grimy corners, they longed for a bath and clean clothing. No one had bathed in days nor changed their clothing. Washing wasn't a priority. Survival was the only thing on the agenda.

Some of the passengers sat on the straw, some leaned against the slats on the sides, and some remained standing, but all looked worn out. Everyone was quiet. All waited for the magic moment when an engine would come, attach their boxcar to a train, and move along with it. It could be hours or days before this happened, or it even could be moments.

During the night, that same night, it happened. A steam locomotive jarred the car, attached itself, and then pulled the car out of the station. The steam engine maneuvered the boxcar along the squeaky tracks until it reached a wide-open space in the train yard. There it placed the boxcar at the end of a long train. Relief and hope mixed with fear again crept into the group. Perhaps this would be the first step to safety or the first step to something worse.

Slowly, the trail of boxcars moved along the tracks. As the speed picked up, the chilly night air crept into the already cold car. Even though the boxcar was filled with people, the bodies did not generate enough heat to warm the space. The stove could only be used at times when it was sure the smoke could not be detected. During the night, the fire was lit. The light from the stove flickered into the thick darkness as everyone waited for the warmth to reach them. At first it was hard to sleep, but soon the rhythm of the tracks and the warmer air soothed everyone. Some of the travelers slept, some just sat and stared into space, and some fed the wood stove. The fire was allowed to go out long before the first ray of light touched the boxcar.

Clacking along the tracks, the train traveled past fields, dark woods, and bombed-out villages. The view from the car was very limited because only small cracks in the siding let in the light. Periodically, the rhythm of the train would change. The clacking of the rails would slow down and then stop. Boxcars would be unlatched, rearranged, and attached to different trains. The train would then continue. Throughout the night and next day, the train clacked along at its own gait, sometimes fast, sometimes at a snail's pace. Then the train suddenly stopped.

For a while, no one moved—just listened. Outside, all was quiet—no human voices. At last, someone peeked through the cracks, then unwired the door and gingerly slid it open just a fraction. The afternoon sun and fresh air poured into the dark musty car. Soon, the door was opened all the way.

Immediately, a flurry of activity occurred. "Stay on the train," Wanda admonished her children as she joined other adults in sliding out of the boxcar and onto the ground. Cooking fires were quickly built. No one knew how long the stop would be so they scurried to prepare the food and cook it before the train left again.

This scenario happened over and over again. Sometimes as the engine hooked up at the front of the long train, no one knew they were moving until the cars started to be jarred. Immediately, there was another scurry of activity. Pans of hot food were pushed onto the straw covered floor as the train started to move. The fire was quickly scattered and everyone ran to catch up with the train. As the train was moving, they hung on to the side and climbed in. It was frightening! Ela always stood in the shadows and nervously watched. Would they all get in before the train picked up speed? Would it leave them behind? Everyone had become like family to her and she was scared for them.

Several times when the train stopped, someone would run to the nearest town to buy food. Food was always an issue. There was never enough to completely quell off the hunger. Whoever ran took an enormous risk. Would they return in time before the train left again?

This type of "shopping" happened several times. As soon as the train stopped, they ran across the fields toward the edge of the woods, and disappeared. Eyes stayed focused on the horizon, waiting for them to return. Fear gripped their hearts as they waited, hoping that they would return in time. Often as the train started to depart, someone raced across the fields toward the big sliding door, reached it, and had help getting on. Each time Ela felt the fear and a knot would form in her chest. It was like a slow motion movie in which one can't quite reach the goal.

One day, three of the men raced toward a village to find food. While they were gone, the steam engine emerged, attached itself to the boxcars, and started to move. Across the field the men raced at break-neck speed. The small door at the end of the car was opened. The men ran on the tracks, toward that door. With anguished faces and outstretched arms they tried to connect with the car. Ela stood nearby, saw their faces, and became extremely distraught. Adults leaned out of the car with outstretched arms, trying to connect with them. None of them made it. It was dreadful! Only God knew if they ever would be reunited with their families.

Fear and anxiety were constant companions. Occasionally, the children would go outside to play but most of the time they stayed in the car. Anxiously they would watch and wait for everyone to be inside again.

Food rations were always meager but now were dangerously low. No one knew how God would supply the next meal.

Early one morning, the train came to a complete stop. Before long a lineman came, unhooked just the one car, and returned to the train. The rest of the train left, leaving the car all alone in the quiet of the morning. Listening for voices, they heard none. Someone peered through the crack in the wooden walls and only saw fields, acres and acres of fields. They were alone in the middle of fields that reached to the horizon. Remnants of potato stalks littered the soil. Apparently this field produced a potato harvest the year before.

Inasmuch as no one appeared to be around, the wire that kept the huge door closed was loosened and the door pushed open ever so slightly. Once they were assured that all was safe, the door was opened wide. Immediately, there was a scurry of activity. Again, the adults jumped off the train, keeping an eye on the horizon and looking for approaching danger. Cooking fires were started but there wasn't much to cook.

When they had a chance to look around, they wondered if a potato or two could have survived the winter. Perhaps there were some under the soil that did not freeze. Perhaps they could dig into the ground and find potatoes to cook and fill their bellies.

In Europe, farmers always stored their winter supply of root vegetables by stacking them on the ground, and covering them with a thick layer of straw and then a thick layer of soil over the whole mound. These mounds were usually stored close to the farmhouse so food would be easily accessible during the winter.

While digging in the field, one of the boxcar travelers spotted a hill, at the edge of the field. He pointed, and others looked at the mound. Quickly, they ran to investigate. As they came closer, they saw that straw was scattered everywhere. Their heart started to race with anticipation. Perhaps this was a potato mound. As they dug into the hill, to their utter amazement a storehouse of potatoes emerged. Quickly, others jumped from the boxcars, ran, and eagerly gathered the potatoes. They gathered the potatoes with such joy, as if they had found gold.

That day everyone had a meal. Everyone had enough to eat. It was wonderful! Wanda's family thanked God for His kindness and for always supplying all their needs.

One day Romek and Danek needed to work off some energy. Wanda gave them permission to play outside. They played hide-and-seek on top, underneath, and around the car. They were enjoying themselves immensely. Romek thought a good hiding place would be in the ice trough on top of the car. He climbed up, squeezed himself inside the trough, and hid. He was very quiet as Danek looked everywhere for him. After a while, Danek got tired of the game and went to watch Wanda cook the food. Meanwhile, while Romek waited to be discovered, he fell asleep.

Without warning, the train started to move. Wanda quickly grabbed Danek and lifted him onto the train. Pushing the food onto the car floor, she climbed in, expecting that Romek would be inside. When she could not find him, she frantically started calling, "Romek, Romek. Where are you?" Immediately, everyone started looking for him. Should she leave the train and look for her son or should she stay with her two younger children? "God!" she pleaded, "what shall I do?" She looked out the back door and could not see him. By this time, the train was accelerating. Holding on to the side of the door, she leaned out and wondered if she should jump.

"Romek, Romek!" she frantically called again.

Just then, she heard a voice from above. "Mama, I'm here!" It was Romek's voice, but she could not see him. She wondered if she had just imagined it or if that really was her son. Her frantic calls woke him from his sleep. Again, he said, "Mama, I'm up here. I'm in the ice trough."

"Don't move! Stay there!" Wanda admonished with immense relief. There was no way that he could come down into the car safely so he had to ride, encased, until the train stopped again.

Whenever danger was sensed, the boxcar residents prepared for possible inspections. At night, the huge rusty door was wired shut from the *outside* in order to fool the enemy. This was done to make it appear as if the car had been inspected and sealed by the soldiers.

One night the train stopped in a large train station. This night, like no other night, would forever be emblazoned in Ela's being. This night would be one of the most defining moments of her young life. It was a night of horror that she would never forget.

A lot of commotion and clamor woke everyone from their sleep. Wanda pinched her waking children to warn them of danger. Whispering, she said, "If soldiers come, don't talk, don't answer any questions." They were all very quiet–just waiting. Shouting, banging, and rifle shots were heard outside of the boxcar as people were dragged out of cars and taken away.

"Czesia, get under the blanket," Anna nervously ordered her daughter as she made a space for her under the heads of her family. Anna worried that if her disabled daughter was taken, she would be severely mistreated. Quickly, Czesia crept under the straw and was covered with the blankets. Everyone lay on top of her, pretending she was just a pillow.

As they waited in utter silence, the banging and shooting came closer and closer. Yelling, pleading, screaming, and rifle fire filled the night. Boxcars were ripped opened. Piles of straw were tested for humanity with bayonets. Wanda's children knew that this was the time to be quieter than they had ever been before–no whispering, no whimpering, no moving. Absolutely no moving–not even breathing.

Soon, rifle butts rammed the sides and doors of the car next to theirs. Angry voices yelled and fists pounded the sides of the car. The huge doors were ripped open and the inhabitants, at gunpoint, were taken away.

The children were not sure what was happening, but Wanda knew, and always knew what to do–she prayed. "Father in heaven, help us! Please let them pass us by, but if not, then please give me wisdom to know what to do and what to say."

Everyone held their breath as the banging started on the sides of their boxcar. The cutting of the outside wires followed the banging and shouting. The huge sliding door was forced open, exposing all inside. They were found out!

Wanda held her children close as one by one, at gunpoint, adults were ordered to get off the train. Soon, just Wanda's family was left. Pointing at Zosia, a soldier ordered her off the train. "But I have a baby!" she exclaimed as she held Jagoda tightly in her arms.

"Don't play games with me," the soldier replied. "Give her back to her mother," he said, pointing his rifle in Wanda's direction.

"That is her daughter," Anna confirmed.

"I don't believe you. Give the child back to her mother," he repeated angrily as he again pointed at Wanda.

What could Zosia do? Putting Jagoda in Wanda's arms, with silent tears pouring down her face, she left. Wanda's children stared in utter shock.

Next, a soldier pointed his rifle at Anna and told her to get off. Didn't he see that she was a grandmother? Didn't he realize that she was too old and feeble to be useful? Slowly, she stood. With her head bent forward, she walked to the edge of the boxcar. She glanced briefly at her family as a soldier grabbed her by the elbow, and pulled her onto the ground.

No good-byes were permitted, no hugs or kisses, not even a touch or a prayer. They disappeared into the night. Wanda, Czesia, and the children were left with just the hot tears that burned in their eyes and the screams that were stuck in their throats, not knowing if they would ever see their loved ones again.

Zosia and Anna joined a crowd of people that were herded, like cattle, into different groups. Armed soldiers were poised in case anyone tried to escape. All detainees were waiting to be taken to different manual work projects. Both Zosia and Anna were taken to different areas of the station.

Wanda, the children, and Czesia still in hiding, were now alone in the boxcar. Wanda was young and very spry. She would have been a good catch for whatever purpose they intended. But because she had children, by the grace of God, she was spared.

Somehow God gave her the strength, fortitude, courage, and boldness to do what she did next. Not letting things stand as they were, the thought came to her that she should go and find her mother and sister. Sensing that the soldiers spared her because she had children, she took an enormous risk. She felt confident that the Lord would be with her and would help her as He had so many times before.

Leaving Jagoda in Romek and Danek's care and Czesia still under the straw, she took Ela by the hand and led her into the terror of the night. How could she leave the children and Czesia alone? If she didn't return, who would care for them? Was Czesia capable of caring for them and herself? But Wanda was determined to search for her mother and her sister.

Into the dim light of the train station, she ventured. Over railroad tracks, around boxcars, and between soldiers she searched for her loved ones. Crowds of people were everywhere. Wanda's eyes scanned the groups as her eyes darted from face to face. She was so intent on searching that she wasn't even aware that she was holding Ela's hand.

Incredibly, as she milled in and out among the detained groups and soldiers, she was not stopped. There were more and more tracks to cross. Ela was exhausted and scared, and the tracks became hard to maneuver. Wanda let go of her hand and climbed on top of boxcars to get a better view. On the ground, Ela followed as Wanda jumped from one car to another. Not finding them, she jumped down, took Ela's hand again, and continued looking.

Even with her childish intellect, Ela knew she had to pretend that what they were doing was normal and that they belonged where they were walking. She must not cry out or show any emotion. She must not call attention to herself or her mother. For her anxious, exhausted mother, who was moving and walking in a nightmare, it was impossible to be aware of everything in her surroundings. It was impossible for her to shield Ela's childish eyes from inappropriate sights. Wanda's eyes were lifted high, darting here and there, trying to catch a glimpse of her mother and sister.

Just as they rounded the corner of a railroad car, Ela recoiled and gasped as she clutched her mother's hand even tighter. Her eyes saw something that no child should see. Had circumstances been different, even then, Wanda would have seen it first and diverted her attention. "Look away," she would have said and, "don't look down." Ela knew what that meant, and would have obeyed. Wanda had said that to her children many times before. But right now her eyes were on a different plane. She was looking for two precious faces in a sea of faces that were dimly lit. She did not see what Ela saw.

There, on the tracks, lay the body of a man on his back, split wide open with his intestines spread in all directions. Even in the dim light, Ela saw everything, including the large puddles of blood. Wanda did not even notice as they stepped over and in the remains. Her eyes were intensely searching for Anna and Zosia. Ela knew she must not cry out! She must not scream! She must not cry out! She must act as if she is unaffected by this scene. She must not call attention to them. She kept holding on tightly to her mother's hand as they continued searching.

Miraculously, Wanda found Anna in a group getting ready to board a train for a work camp. Without hesitation, she boldly approached one of the guards and said, "That lady over there, she is much too old and weak to work. She will only slow you down. Why don't you let her go?" The soldier looked at Anna. Hunched over with her head bowed down, she looked very frail. He motioned her out of the group, looked her over again, and dismissed her. Relieved, Wanda quickly took Anna back to the boxcar home and took Ela out again into the night.

After searching further, God provided another miracle. Wanda found Zosia. She was with another group preparing to board a string of boxcars.

Again, Wanda boldly approached a guard. "Did you notice that she is crippled and can hardly walk?" Wanda spoke confidently and firmly pointing at Zosia. "With that leg she will hinder the other workers and will slow them down."

Why did this guard even listen to her? Who would he have to answer to if he let a prisoner go? The soldier pondered her words for a moment then, pointing at Zosia, said, "Hey you, come over here." Zosia, who had broken her leg a few months earlier, limped slowly toward him. He looked at her and said, "Let me see you walk." She limped even more profusely as he watched.

"Get out of here!" he growled. Slowly, she limped toward Wanda and, with Wanda and Ela, disappeared into the darkness.

They were all together again in the boxcar—safe. There, on their knees, embracing each other, they thanked God for His protection, His guidance, and His mercy.

Chapter 20

Secure in His Care

You will keep in perfect peace all who trust in you, whose thoughts are fixed on you! Trust in the Lord always, for the Lord God is the eternal Rock.

—Isaiah 26:3–4

Minutes ticked by, then hours. Wanda's family was alone in the boxcar, listening for footsteps and expecting more danger. Carefully, the large door was pulled shut and the darkness enshrouded them once again. They tried to sleep.

On the platform, the noise continued. The detainees were loaded onto trains; the huge doors of each car closed and bolted shut. None of those encased had a say in what their destiny would be. They just waited. The trains quickly moved out of the station and departed. The roundup was over. With the crowds of prisoners gone, the soldiers also disbursed. The night became quiet.

Everything happened so quickly and yet it seemed as if in slow motion! *Did this really happen or was it just a horrible nightmare?* Wanda's mind questioned. In her exhaustion, she closed her eyes and slumped down onto the straw. As if in unison, the boys crawled up next to her. Romek put his arm around his mother and whispered, "Everything will be all right, Mama." Immediately, Ela was there, clinging to her mother and would not let go. Anna, still trembling, sat next to Czesia while Zosia, clutching her baby, sat motionless and just stared. The night passed. They stayed in the boxcar.

As dawn approached, the sisters and their mother rose from a fitful sleep. How unmerciful human beings can be to each other! How merciful God is to have rescued them again.

What to do next? Where to go? Where was it safe? The war was over, but why was this horror still occurring? Would this train continue on its way to more horror or would it just stay in this station? "Dear Lord Jesus, show me where to go and what to do next," Wanda prayed.

"I'll be right back," Wanda said as she rose from the straw. "We need to know where this train is going."

Recalling the events of the night before, she decided to again take Ela with her. Gently, she nudged her daughter and softly spoke, "Ela, wake up. We have to go on a mission." Ela woke and looked at her mother. Traumatized from what she had seen, she immediately grasped her mothers' hand, clung to it, and together they went into the quiet, misty morning. The quietness of the morning was a mocking contrast to the noisy anguish of the shadowy hours that will forever hang in their memories. Hastily, they went to the stationmaster and within minutes returned. "This train is staying in this station," Wanda announced, "but another one will take us close to Września. It will leave later this morning."

They left the boxcar, walked across the platform, and entered a train that consisted of a row of cattle cars. Wanda recalled the comfortable trains of the past with windows, leather seats, small compartments with a door on each end, and a long hallway running the length of the car. The conductor would walk the corridor and enter each compartment as he collected the tickets. Perhaps some day they would again ride in such luxury, but for now, this was their way to get home. At last, they now were heading in the right direction, closer to the home they left the day after Wanda's birthday.

Mid-morning, the train left the horror-filled station, the station that just hours before was filled with anguish, tears, rifles, and pain. Wanda's family again was grateful that God had intervened and kept them together. They were grateful to still be alive, grateful that they would soon be home in comforting surroundings, and grateful that soon they would be sleeping in their beds and doing the ordinary, simple, wonderful things of life.

By late afternoon, the cattle car train arrived at a small station. This was as close as this train would get to Września. They still had to transfer to another train before they could reach their goal. Gathering up their bundles and the baby buggy, they disembarked. At last, hope was in sight. Only a few more hours, and they would be safe, home again.

Unfortunately, once they talked to the stationmaster, he informed them that the next train would depart in five days. Five days? What a shock! What a disappointment! Standing together on the platform, they looked lost. There were no restaurants, no hotels, no venders selling food, nothing, just signs of the ravages of war. Everywhere they went, they saw destruction. This station was no exception.

"Mama, I'm hungry," Danek grimaced as he looked at his mother.

"I know, dear," Wanda replied, not knowing where the next morsels of food would come from. The children were always hungry and it tore her up when she had nothing to give them. She often fasted and gave her food to her children. "In a little while we'll see if we can find something to eat," she promised.

A few soldiers were milling around with the travelers but at least not huge companies of soldiers, marching in cadence, filling travelers with fear.

"Look, Mama, what is that?" Ela said as she pointed with surprise. In the distance, perched on the shoulder of a soldier, was a large green parrot. The children were astonished to see such a large bird. They had never been to a zoo and had never seen such a large, beautifully colored bird.

A Russian soldier started walking toward them and immediately the children froze with fear. Closer and closer he came until he stood directly in front of them. Smiling, he said, "Would you like to stroke the parrot?" They didn't answer. "He won't bite you." He stooped down to the children's level and started to talk to the bird. The parrot chattered back as if it knew what the soldier was saying. Slowly, the children overcame their fear and took interest in this amazing sight.

Still stooping, he pulled out a large flat package from inside his jacket. "Would you like some bread?" he asked. The children looked at Wanda and then refused. "It's all right," he whispered. "I'm a Christian." He pulled a cross out from under his uniform to prove what he was saying was true. Immediately, he tucked it back under his chin and hid it. "Please take the bread," he said with sincerity in his eyes. Again, the children looked at Wanda for approval. Wanda thanked the soldier and gave her children permission to take the slices of bread.

Pleased that he could help, the soldier left with the beautiful bird still perched on his shoulder, chattering away. The Russian sauntered down the platform till he was out of sight.

What a wonderful sight! What a wonderful gift! Romek, Danek, and Ela immediately shared the bread and eagerly devoured it.

Wanda's family continued standing on the platform, still wondering where to go. Where could they take shelter for the night and the next few days?

All of a sudden, across the station on the next platform, loud, angry voices could be heard. Soldiers, approaching a pregnant woman, started arguing with her. She argued back. Within moments the commotion turned into furious exchanges, then screaming.

"Children, don't look that way! Turn away!" Wanda demanded emphatically as she pulled them farther away from the scene.

The loud arguing increased until it became an unearthly scream. Seconds later, the woman begged, "Kill me! Kill me!" Wanda glanced in her direction and saw a horrendous sight. The woman was holding her belly as blood poured from a ghastly gaping wound. In his anger, a soldier had bayoneted her and her unborn child. She was in such agony that she was begging someone, anyone, to kill her. The soldiers just walked away.

The screaming continued as Wanda and her family ran to the other end of the station, as far away as they could from her tormented cries.

In a frenzy, they ran into a small bombed-out building that used to be the train depot. Quickly, they found a corner and hid. The windows were broken. Rubble and glass covered the floor, but they were glad to be out of sight. This certainly was not a place for children or any human being but what choices were there right now? They hid and waited.

Wanda continually carried on a conversation with the One she loved, the Lord Jesus. He was the One she always turned to for help and comfort. He was her friend, her guide, her Savior, and her companion in the best of times and in the darkest times. Again, she talked to Him. "Dear Jesus, I'm so scared! Please be with that woman who was hurt. You know what happened. Please do what needs to be done to help her. Be with us also. Please keep danger away from us. You can see what conditions we are in right now. It's just not safe to stay here. Is it possible to have a better place to sleep tonight? You know how hard I'm trying to help my family. I'm really tired. We all are tired and need to rest. You always know what we need, dear Lord. You know even before we ask. Do You hear me tonight?" She waited. "I know You hear me."

As she prayed, a strong thought came into her mind. The next person that comes out of a building will be a sign for them. That is the building they are to go to. "Did I understand You correctly, Lord? The next person we see leaving a building is a sign for us to take shelter there?" She meditated on that thought for a moment and was convinced that this was a sign from the Lord.

It wasn't long before a soldier exited a building that was practically across from the station. Without hesitation, the whole family walked across the street and into the building.

The two-story building was large with a lot of rooms, almost like a mansion. There was no furniture, none at all, but there were windows and doors, walls without holes, and a roof. They felt blessed. Cautiously, they listened, then tiptoed across a room and sat down under the window sash where if someone should look through the window, they would not be detected. They kept listening. It was absolutely silent.

As the light started to fade, Wanda and Zosia went to inspect the building. They tiptoed from room to room. Every room was empty. Carefully, they crept up the stairs. All the rooms up there were also empty. The whole house continued to be absolutely silent. Next, they checked the basement. Gingerly, they crept down to the foot of the stairs, waited, and listened.

What was that? Shivers went down their spines. They heard the sounds again. Could that be rat noises? Frozen in place, they waited. Seconds later, shadows came out of the darkness. Three women approached them and whispered, "You scared us! We thought you were Russian soldiers." Wanda and Zosia, in unison, gasped a sigh of relief and started up a friendly conversation.

The three middle-aged women were also waiting for a train, a train that would depart the next day. They shared some information about what they had discovered during their delay.

"Behind the building, there's an abandoned garden. The weeds are very tall, but food is stored there. Look among the weeds, you'll find a pile of soil. That's where it is." Potatoes and root vegetables had been piled up, and covered with straw and then a thick layer of soil.

"You said you have children? There's a goat tethered in the garden. The poor thing was bleating for hours, begging to be milked. No one came, so we milked it."

"Another thing," one of the women informed, "there are a few pots in the kitchen and some wood in the back, but wait till it's dark to use the stove just in case."

What incredible news. What an answer to prayer. This was like staying in a wonderful lodge. The sisters went back to the family and shared the first "ray of sunshine" they had seen in days.

Czesia went out with Wanda, milked the goat, and came back inside to share the abundance.

As darkness approached, they all settled down to sleep on the floor next to the wall under the window. Although exhausted, Anna could not sleep. Instead, she quietly rested and listened. As she listened, she heard two sets of footsteps parading down the street. A soft female voice spoke and a Russian male voice responded. The footsteps stopped in front of a building across the street. The male voice whistled. After a pause, he whistled again. Moments later someone answered from inside that building with a different whistling pattern. It appeared to be a signal. The set of footsteps continued down the street without entering the building. Anna heard this whistling pattern several times as the hours passed by.

Without straw, the floor was hard and sleep would not come to Anna. She continued to rest in the stillness, but still could not sleep. Once more she heard footsteps. Again she heard two sets of footsteps, a heavy step and a lighter one, probably a soldier with his girlfriend looking for a private corner for the rest of the night. The footsteps came closer and closer and stopped directly in front of Anna's window.

The soldier whistled in the familiar pattern she had heard several times during the night. He whistled again, waiting for the response that would indicate that the building was occupied. There was silence.

With her heart pounding, Anna took a deep breath and whistled a loud response, a copy of the one she had heard. Immediately, everyone under the windowsill was awake. Quickly, she quieted them. The footsteps left and continued down the street to another building.

Morning came. The family woke with new hope, knowing that on this day there would be vegetables provided from the garden and more milk for the children. *There must be bread available somewhere in this town,* Wanda thought. She took Ela with her to investigate the possibility. As they walked along the street, hungry people searched for food among the garbage discarded by the side of the road. One woman gathered potato peels and placed them in her apron.

While they were gone, a stray cow wandered down the street and stopped almost in front of the building where Wanda's family was staying. Several Russian soldiers corralled the cow and killed it. Immediately they dressed the animal, cut it up, and left the entrails lying on the street. They took the meat and disappeared.

As soon as they were gone, Cześia and Anna ran into the street, gathered up the tripe (cow's stomach), and brought it into the back yard. In the yard, they found a large oval tin tub, and filled it with water. Washing the heavy, leathery tripe was exhausting. Zosia, Czesia and Anna all helped with the washing. Over and over they washed the tripe, trying to rid it of the undigested grass. When Wanda returned, she too helped as her children watched. They watched the white honeycomb tripe floating in the water, being washed, until it was ready to be cut up and cooked.

The next few days there was an abundance of food. All of it, of course, was tripe soup with vegetables, but it was wonderfully filling, and no one complained.

And so it was, until it was time to board the train and ride the remaining miles to Września.

Chapter 21

Unsettling Peace

"For the mountains may depart and the hills disappear, but even then I will remain loyal to you. My covenant of blessing will never be broken," says the Lord, who has mercy on you.

—Isaiah 54:10

The train ride to Września was uneventful except for the fact that this train was a passenger train with seats, people sized doors, windows, and, wonder of wonders, a civilized place called a lavatory. This train felt very luxurious. The children sat mesmerized, their eyes glued to the cavalcade of scenes that passed by the windows. They felt as if they were on an amusement park ride. Joy tickled within them. This was more fun than they had had in months. Wanda leaned back, shut her eyes, and felt very blessed to be sitting on a seat and not cross-legged in the straw of a boxcar. The rest of her family—her Mother, Zosia, Czesia, and baby Jagoda—surrounded her and they were all safe and healthy. She had much for which to be thankful.

The ride ended too soon for the children but not soon enough for the women. At last, with hopes escalating, they arrived in Września, the city they had left behind in January. Unfortunately, everything was not as they had left it. Although some buildings were damaged, they were not totally destroyed, but what was worse, armed Russian soldiers were milling around everywhere. The atmosphere was threatening and intimidating.

From the station they took a *doroszka* (a horse-drawn buggy) to the comfortable apartment they left behind. The family couldn't wait to be reunited with their home, their safe dwelling with rooms, walls, glass windows, beds, kitchen, and the pantry of food they had left behind. The apartment contained so many things they had all missed: Zosia's wedding trousseau, Jagoda's cradle, photographs, Wanda's hand-crafted furniture from Turek, the boys' toy castle, Ela's dolls and doll buggy, the toys Uncle Leon had made, and all the other creature comforts. Wanda remembered her birthday celebration and the wonderful half eaten tort. She wondered what it might look like after all these months.

At last, they were standing in front of their door. Everyone watched as Zosia searched for her key. She bumped the door slightly and, to her surprise, the door moved. The door was unlocked! She was sure she had locked it before they left. Everyone watched as she pushed the door wide open. Their smiles immediately turned into utter shock. No one could move. The whole apartment was ransacked.

Walking around the apartment in silence, they just shook their heads in disbelief. Nearly all the furniture was gone. Embroidered bedding and tablecloths, toys, cradle, clothes, food, nearly everything of value was missing. A few things remained, scattered around the apartment. Their hearts sank.

What could they do now? Should they stay here or go somewhere else? "Let's just stay here for now," Zosia advised. "We will assess what is left and decide what to do next." And so they did.

The next few days they felt the atmosphere of fear in the new Września. The city had indeed changed. Russian soldiers were everywhere, their friends and acquaintances were nowhere to be seen, and a wave of uncertainty hung over the city.

They gathered up their belongings, saved a few items, and sold the rest. Wanda was grateful that she could retrieve a few family photographs and the little vest she had made for Ela. The black velvet vest was part of a Polish costume. Wanda loved to embroider and she had spent a lot of time embroidering the brightly colored flowers. Tiny beads and sequins added sparkle that a little girl could not resist. Only a few other items were worth saving—some yards of material, a dress Wanda had embroidered before her wedding, and a few other miscellaneous items.

The decision was made to move away from this Russian-occupied city and move to a quieter place, a little village close to the German border. They had heard friends speak lovingly of a little village called Jabłonowo. They hoped that it was still a safe place to work, live, and raise a family.

A few days later, they arrived in Jabłonowo. The little gathering of houses did look peaceful and picturesque, just as their friends had described. The lane was lined with beautiful, blossoming cherry trees. It took their breath away. A country lane wound its way among the farms and houses to a one-room schoolhouse at the edge of the village. It then continued through the fields that soon would be planted with cabbages, grains, sugar beets, and potatoes.

Without too much effort, they found work and a little cottage to rent. Life again started to look hopeful. The furnished, thatched-roof cottage was small, but certainly adequate for this family of eight. The house was divided into four little rooms, all on one level. Three of the rooms were for living, the other one for storage. The three rooms had wooden floors. The fourth room had a mud floor.

The sparsely furnished kitchen had a wood-burning stove, a sink with a hand pump for water, a table, chairs, and a daybed. One bedroom was furnished with a double bed and a wardrobe. The other bedroom contained two double beds, a table, and a trap door under the table that led to a cold storage cellar under the house. Curtains hung over the windows and over the glass doors that divided the rooms.

The main entrance into the house was in the kitchen. The entrance consisted of an alcove bracketed with two sets of sturdy doors, one on the outside, the other on the kitchen side.

The accommodations were ample, actually luxurious by the standards of the last few months. Excitement filled the family and they began to smile again. At last, a place they could call home.

In short order they purchased whitewash and whitewashed all the walls. In the two bedrooms they even decorated the walls using a rubber roller with a flower design. They dipped the roller in maroon paint and ran it down the wall in a ribbon design. The place was becoming their own.

A waist-high white picket fence surrounded the perimeter of the yard. The yard was divided into two sections. To the right of the house was the main entrance, a garden section, and at the far edge of the property, a large storage shed that housed the outhouse. The left side of the property was comprised of two large wooden structures: a huge barn and a large shed. They housed several stray cats and, without a doubt, a colony of mice. Along the back edge of the yard, water ran in a small ditch that carried it to the well just outside the kitchen window. This well gathered the water that was then pumped into the house at the kitchen sink.

One more thing: at the back of the property, a tall concrete wall secured an apple orchard that, since the occupation, belonged to the Russian military. No one was to enter–it was forbidden.

Aside from the wall, this house had everything. What more could they ask for? The women felt blessed to have such comfortable accommodations and work so they now could buy food and necessities. They were settling in and thanking God for His care and kindness.

Throughout the seasons they worked on the farms and in the fields. They fed animals, cleaned pens, did sewing and mending for the farmers, cooked for the farmhands and farm family, and cleaned the houses and yards. They worked in the fields gathering potatoes and sugar beets. They gathered grain for the farmers, brought it back to their farms, and threshed it on the barn floor with a threshing tool. When they had saved enough money, they bought a goat, chickens, and seven geese; one of the geese was blind.

The work was hard, but rewarding. Food now was available and adequate. After gleaning grain for themselves, they ground it in a coffee grinder till it became flour. As larger amounts were gleaned, the grain was put into a sack and taken to the mill.

A garden was planted. The soil was good and the produce grew well. All the tomato plants thrived. One of the plants, however, was amazing. It flourished like no other they had ever seen. This plant grew and grew until it had to be supported by wooden poles. The tomatoes hung in clusters, like grapes. By the end of the season, this plant had produced three hundred and sixty good-sized tomatoes. It was amazing! Everyone in the neighborhood was astonished! It was said that there had been a rotten tree on that spot, but no one could explain why this tomato plant was so prolific.

Many chores occupied the lives of the children. At six years of age, Ela learned to peel potatoes. Since potatoes were a daily mainstay, she became quite proficient as she helped the women in this repeated task. Whenever the adults sat with her and chatted while working, she felt important.

Another chore that Ela enjoyed was making butter. Cream was poured into a wooden butter churn and a wooden paddle was inserted through a hole in the lid. The paddle would move up and down, up and down until the cream turned into lovely clumps of light yellow butter. The butter was strained out of the liquid and placed into an enameled tin bowl. The liquid was saved for drinking or for cooking.

The seven geese were also Ela's responsibility. She loved taking them out to new pastures and watching them as they waddled, following each other through the tall grasses. The blind goose followed in close pursuit, not realizing it had a handicap. However, Ela didn't like to watch when the geese were force-fed to fatten them up. *Kluski* (long dumplings made of flour, egg, and water) were made and forced down the throats of these birds. No one ever told her that these geese would be dinner some day.

Eight-year-old Danek and Romek, not yet ten, also helped with chores. It was their duty to care for the goat and the chickens. They also helped in the fields. They gathered grain, potatoes, and the large sugar beets. Ela also accompanied the family as they went to work in the fields.

At the end of the day, the horse-drawn wagons were piled high with grain or root vegetables. The boys would shimmy up on top and ride back to the village pretending to be conquering heroes. Ela often rode in a small wagon hitched to the back of the giant wagon. Her legs would stick out from between the slats on the side.

One day, as the entourage was returning to the village, the little wagon tipped over with Ela's legs trapped underneath. The skin on one leg was severely scraped. When they got home, Anna washed the wound, found a flat leafed herb growing close to the ground, washed the leaf, and applied it to the wounds. This was used as an antibiotic. The only ointments for wounds available at that time were zinc oxide and a thick black paste to draw out infections, but neither of those were available in this household. Ela was glad that Anna did not apply the aqua sulfur powder into her wounds. She remembered how Danek writhed when it was applied to infections on his legs. Ela continued going to the fields, even as her wound was healing.

The work in the fields was hard, but it provided money to buy food and supplies. The available food was simple but adequate and good. A favorite meal was clabbered milk and boiled potatoes. Milk was left in a container overnight to sour. It became thick, creamy, and tart.

A comfort food for the children was milk soup, which was served for breakfast. Most of the time it was thickened with flour and a little butter, and eaten with a slice of bread. Milk soup was also good served with dumplings. The milk was heated to boiling. Next, small lumps of dough were dropped into the hot milk. This also was eaten with a slice of bread.

Between-meal snacks were unheard of, but if hunger really persisted, a dry piece of bread or an apple filled the need. Occasionally, however, Anna would take a piece of cold, boiled potato, hold it in her hand, and apply a dollop of jam on the top.

One day, Danek decided that he would make pancakes. Most things that he did, he did very well. He made the batter exactly right and started to fry it in some grease. His confidence grew, but only for a moment. All of a sudden, the pan burst into flames. He stared at the flames as they rose higher and higher. He panicked and didn't know what to do.

Next to the stove, clothes were soaking in a washtub. With his heart pounding, he lifted the flaming pan and plunged it into the tub full of clothes. That was the end of the fire, the pancakes, and his confidence. What did he do wrong? He wasn't sure.

The days passed. In the fall of 1945, the brothers started attending school in the one-room schoolhouse. The teacher was sweet and they enjoyed school. Attending school gave them an opportunity to be with other children and make friends. The brothers started to relax and behave as normal boys–mischievous.

The tall concrete wall protecting the Russian orchard caught their attention and became a challenge. As the fruit ripened, it beckoned them till it became impossible to resist. As the brothers played with their friends, they plotted together to conquer the wall and come back with the "spoils of war." The danger was real to the conquering heroes but with prodding and dares from the others, they continued plotting.

Their plan worked for a while but did not end well. The apples were wonderful and some found their way to different boys' homes. Wanda appreciated the apples her sons brought home, but did not question them. Fruit trees lined the lane and were there for anyone to use. In the spring, Ela loved to sit in the trees and feast on the luscious ripe cherries. The boys did the same. No one objected. Apples were also available for the taking. The trees were dispersed throughout the countryside, but the Russian apple orchard was off limits.

One day, as they jumped over the concrete wall, a Russian soldier yelled at the intruders. Quick as spry deer, they jumped back over the wall and ran home. The soldier ran in pursuit along the opposite side of the tall concrete wall.

"I know where you live! You wait, you hooligans," he shouted over the wall. "My commandant will come and take care of you. You'll be sorry!" he yelled.

Sure enough, in a little while, the Russian commandant arrived with the soldier accompanying him. "Over there! That's where they live," he shouted. They knocked on the door and waited.

Living in the country, Wanda had regained her strength and feistiness and was not afraid of the Russian soldiers. After all, the war was over. She removed her apron, straightened her hair, and opened the door. Sweetly, she said, "Can I help you?"

Gruffly, the handsome commandant inquired, "Do you have sons?"

"Yes, two young sons," Wanda answered, looking directly into the commandant's eyes.

His voice softened. "I understand that your sons were in our orchard stealing apples."

"What? I know nothing about that. We have lots of apple trees in our area. Why would they take your apples?"

Just then, Ela came to the door and leaned against her mother's skirt.

"Is that your little girl?" the commandant quipped. He leaned down and chucked the blond girl under the chin and said, "You're a pretty little thing."

Ela smiled and shyly turned away.

He stood up, looked directly at Wanda, and said, "Anyway, don't let it happen again. That wall is there for a reason. Tell them to stay away. We don't want any trouble."

Without an ounce of intimidation, Wanda lifted her chin and said, "Thank you. I'll make sure they don't go anywhere near your wall. Thank you for your visit, Commandant."

With that, he turned and the two soldiers walked toward the picket fence. The commandant stopped, turned, and glanced at Wanda once more, then returned to his compound. From then on, the commandant found every opportunity he could to walk past the house and stop and greet Wanda. He tried to befriend the children by speaking kindly to them and showing interest in their activities.

As the weeks and months passed, he continued showing kindness to Wanda. He obviously was fond of her and wanted her to feel the same for him. One day, he found Wanda tending her garden. Stepping into the yard, he walked over to a stool and sat down. "You are working too hard. It troubles me to see you struggling day after day. Aren't you tired of it all?"

"I'm all right," Wanda replied. "My hands are still strong and so far I've been healthy."

"Stop a moment and listen," he urgently said. "Come and sit down. I want to tell you something."

Wanda looked at him, wondering why his voice had changed, and walked toward where he pointed.

"I've been watching you for a long time. You are a fine woman. I have some money and would like to take care of you and your children. Would you marry me?" he pleaded as he looked at her.

For a moment, Wanda sat in shock, pondering what he had just said. She had not expected those words but she knew how to answer. "I'm sorry. I am married. Someday my husband will return and we will be a family again."

"Your husband must have been killed. So many have died. It's an impossible dream to think that he is still alive. If he were alive, he would have found you by now," he said earnestly, looking at her face. "I love you, Wanda. Marry me!"

"I can't. My husband *will* return!" she said emphatically. "Thank you, commandant, for your kindness," Wanda said as she lowered her head. "I am flattered by your offer, but I really can not accept."

The commandant stood and quietly said, "I will wait. You will see." As he walked away he uttered, "Let me know when you have changed your mind. I will be waiting."

As the months passed, many times the commandant passed by the cottage and exchanged pleasantries. They spoke, but never again on this subject.

Unsettling Peace

Without bombs falling and rifle fire, life in post-war Jabłonowo became almost normal and predictable, but there was always an undertow of fear, fear of the unknown and of what might be. The boys went to school. All three children did chores, helped in the fields, and played with their friends.

Ela found a friend and was glad to spend time with her. Janka took her around the neighborhood, and showed her all the favorite haunts and secret places to gather berries and where the tastiest fruit trees lived. She had a friend at last, someone to spend time with, someone to share secrets and girl talk. It was always exciting to be with Janka because she was full of ideas, some of them, unfortunately, not the best.

One day Janka thought it would be fun to steal eggs from a neighbor's chicken coop. Could they do it without being caught? "Let's wait until they are eating supper," Janka advised. "Their table is in front of the window. We can see them from the street. Then we can sneak under the window and into their yard. We'll be out of there in a flash."

Arm in arm, the friends walked past the farmhouse and up a little hill in front of the window. Yes, there they were, eating supper. Turning around, still arm in arm, they made their way back down the hill, toward the little house.

Once they were out of sight, bending low, they crept under the window. Janka led and Ela followed. Still bending low, they crept toward the chicken coop. Once inside, they quickly each took an egg and retraced their steps. With hearts pounding, they ran till they were out of sight and felt safe. Did the prank succeed?

Now what to do with the egg? Cupping the egg in both her hands, Ela took it to her mother, who was working in the yard. "Look, Mama. Look what I found!" she said as she handed the egg to her mother. It did not take long for Wanda to detect the misdeed. Ela had to return the egg and apologize. This would not be a pleasant memory for Ela, but a lesson well learned.

One day, Romek and two older friends were playing in a field. Discovering a large shell buried in the soil, they dug it up and took it to the back of a barn. They planned to disassemble it. Romek had seen one before. He remembered the incident in Annaberg and the warning. "You better put it down and leave it alone!" he warned. "My grandma said that the shell could explode and kill you."

"Your grandma?" the friends mocked. "What does she know?" They continued laughing at Romek. They found a nail and started to pick at the shell. Romek left and went home.

It wasn't long after Romek returned home that a large explosion shook the countryside. No one left the house to investigate. Memories of shellings and bombings unnerved them. Fear kept them home.

The next day at work, Wanda heard what happened. One of the boys was holding the shell tightly against his body. As he picked at it with that nail, the shell exploded. Before the boy died, as his friend watched, with the stumps of his arms, he tried to push his intestines back into his body. The other boy survived, but was badly hurt.

Occasionally during the night things occurred that frightened everyone and had them cowering in their homes. Just as the Nazis perpetrated many of their crimes under the cover of night, the Russian soldiers did likewise.

One night as the family slept quietly, loud banging startled them. Everyone immediately sat up and listened. Anna ran from her day bed in the kitchen to join the others. "What was that?" Anna whispered as she trembled. The banging continued. Soldiers were outside of the cottage talking loudly and banging against the door.

"Open the door!" they yelled as rifle buts rammed against the front door. Quickly, Wanda's family ran to the back bedroom and huddled together.

"Open the door or we'll break it down!" they yelled as they continued battering the heavy door.

"Oh, Lord, not again!" Wanda prayed. "Must we continually live in fear? Please help us, Lord!"

The yelling and pounding continued, but it had no effect on the sturdy front door. The door held tight. What did they want? Why were they attacking at night? Why were they attacking at all? The war was over. They kept on ramming the door. The windows were glass. They easily could have broken a window and entered that way. Only God knows why that did not happen. Eventually, the soldiers stopped and went to attack another house.

Across the lane an older couple lived alone. A pleasant garden surrounded their cottage. A vegetable garden was planted and was flourishing. The children enjoyed visiting the couple and playing with their kittens and rabbits. They were a peaceful couple, always willing to help in any way they could. When a neighbor died, the wife went to help bathe the deceased and even sewed a shroud. There were no funeral parlors, so everything had to be done at home. The husband was always willing to help local widows by fixing things around their homes. They were truly a congenial couple.

One morning, after a night of commotion and rifle banging, without any explanation they were missing. It was as if they vanished into thin air. Their garden was still flourishing, the rabbits were still in their cages, the chickens were pecking in the yard—but the couple was gone.

Ela stood behind her picket fence, peeking out from behind a bush, and watched as soldiers walked in and out of their cottage. One of them saw Ela and walked over to her. "Here, this is for you. Take care of them," he said as he handed her two of the black rabbits.

Why did he give them to me? Ela wondered. *They belong to our neighbors. I'll keep them till they come back.* They never returned.

It started to become evident that Jablonowo was not the safest place to live. From then on, Wanda felt unsettled. Neighbors gathered in their kitchens and whispered. They talked about Stalin and the horrors that he was perpetrating. The Russians seized the farmers' crops, homes, and belongings. Hundreds and thousands were being arrested, imprisoned, and sent to labor camps. He filled labor camps with peasants who defended their crops and belongings. Thousands of people were being executed. They were even arrested for listening to foreign broadcasts.

The villagers talked a lot and passed around rumors and truths and messages from the Underground. The Underground was a network of people who opposed Hitler and the war and now Stalin and the Communists. During the war, they helped American and British soldiers, the Jews, and others to survive.

They helped by hiding them, helping them escape, smuggling weapons and intelligence information, and helping with communication. They arranged for contact people, safe homes, and passage, and would do whatever was possible to help defectors and the Polish nationals. All this was done usually by word of mouth and at great risk to themselves.

One piece of information that Wanda heard lifted her hopes. She heard of a way some were able to locate missing husbands and sons. It had been months since Józef left. She didn't know where he was or if he was alive. Perhaps he was injured and shut up in a hospital somewhere. Wanda had to find out. She sent a word-of-mouth request to see if they could locate Józef.

A few weeks later, Anna ran excitedly toward Wanda. "Come here! Come to the house. I have some news."

The women rushed home, gathered together with Zosia and Czesia, and waited to hear what the excitement was.

"I have some amazing, *astounding* news! Józef is alive! He's alive and living in England," she stated, gasping for breath as she continued. "Someone from the Underground sent us this message, and there's more."

Wanda could hardly absorb the first piece of news. He was alive? He was alive and living in England? How could that be? This was unbelievable, an answer to prayer.

"He joined the British army and is now in England," Anna continued.

"Does he know that we are alive? Does he know where we are?" Wanda questioned as her mind whirled.

"I don't think so. We'll try to send a message to him and perhaps he'll answer," Anna continued. "But listen, Wanda, I heard something else about the families of British soldiers. I heard that passage to England could be arranged from the British zone of West Germany, but only for immediate family members of British military personnel." (The British zone was in the northern part of Germany.)

This was a lot for Wanda to absorb. *England? British military? Passage? Passage to England? West Germany? Passage to England from the British Zone?* The words spiraled in her mind.

As the hours, days, and weeks passed, she was deep in thought. She waited for a message from Józef. None arrived.

Wanda knew that in Russian-occupied Poland it was illegal to travel without documents. She knew that the consequences could be fatal. No one was allowed out and documents could not be obtained. Even with this knowledge, Wanda made an incredible decision, a decision that would change their lives forever. Why she even entertained such a dangerous thought is hard to imagine. She decided she would take her children out of Poland, across heavily guarded borders, and into the British zone of Germany. Right then, she had no idea how this could be accomplished but she felt that God would be with her and guide her back to her husband.

When I get to the British Zone, I'll contact Józef. I know it's dangerous, but I must go, she mused. *I have to try. I have to find a better life for my children. We were so close to freedom when we were in Germany. If only I had known then. But how can I leave my mother, sisters, and my precious little Jagoda? I love them all so much. I know! When I get there I'll work on papers to bring them to me.* That satisfied her and justified her decision.

As Wanda discussed her decision and secret plans with her mother and sisters, a lull fell over the family. "Why are you doing this?" Anna questioned. "It's just too dangerous."

"Mama, I must–for my children. I must try to give them a better life. When I get to safety, I will bring you to me," she promised. For now, the children were not told of the plans. Everything had to be kept secret. Everything had to look normal.

As her secret plans matured, she felt a need to have a picture taken of the children with Jagoda. She took Ela's Polish costume vest, enlarged it by sewing a patch under the arms and over the shoulder, and made a new skirt. She dressed her sons in their best second-hand clothing and little Jagoda in a sky-blue dress. The not-quite two year old looked so sweet all dressed up, her bright eyes questioning what all the fuss was about. A *doroszka* was hired and off they went to the photographer.

This scenario echoed something familiar. A photo was taken just before Józef left to fight with the Germans, and now a photo was being taken before Wanda and the children were about to leave. Wanda held on to her stomach as an empty feeling welled up inside her. If only they could all leave together!

As fall of 1946 arrived, so did the new school term. At seven and a half, Ela started her first formal education in the one-room schoolhouse. She didn't know that she would only be attending for a very short time. Ela really loved school and especially the gentle teacher. She looked forward to the times that they could walk home together. Being the youngest child in the class made her the teacher's pet. The world was sunny and bright for this young girl.

Wanda looked at the happiness in her daughter's eyes and it made her sad that soon she would have to leave the school and the teacher she loved.

As the time to leave approached, a few last minute decisions had to be made. "How will we know if you are safe?" Zosia asked.

"I won't be able to write a letter because it will be censored. If the Russians find out we are escaping, they might harm you. I know, I'll send you postcards in code," Wanda replied. "I'll pretend that a friend is writing to you from a vacation spot. You will know it's from me."

"Where will you go? Which way will you go? Where will you cross the border?" Anna queried with distress on her face.

"Don't worry, Mama. God will direct us. He will tell us which way to go. I will tell the children that we are going on a little vacation. We first will visit the salt mines in Wieliczka, then possibly we'll travel through the Tetra Mountains. Later on I'll tell them we are going to be with their father. I don't want to scare them. Tomorrow will be the day. Tomorrow morning, we will leave."

Last photo taken before escaping from Poland.
(Jagoda, Ela, Danek and Romek)

Chapter 22

He Will Direct
Your Path

Trust in the Lord with all your heart; do not depend on your own understanding. Seek his will in all you do, and he will direct your paths.

—Proverbs 3:5–6

"Well, good morning children." Wanda cheerfully greeted her children as they sat down for breakfast. "We're going to have an exciting day today."

"Why? What are we going to do?" Romek asked with bewilderment.

"We're going on a little vacation. We're going on a trip to see an amazing place called Wieliczka."

"I've never heard of Wieliczka. What is it? Where is it?" Ela asked, sitting at attention, knowing that it would be just wonderful. If her mother said it, Ela believed her.

"In Wieliczka there is an amazing salt mine. We will go down deep into the earth and see amazing things. There are many rooms made entirely of salt: walls, floor, and ceilings. There is a beautiful cathedral with elaborate sculptures and a chandelier made entirely from salt crystals. There are even three lakes underground. It's something wonderful that you will never forget in your whole life." Wanda tried to make her voice sound excited.

"Are we all going, even Jagoda?" Danek asked.

"No, dear, just the four of us," Wanda replied.

This seemed strange. Their family had done everything together for so long, why not now, the children wondered. Then again, a little vacation would not take long and they would soon be back together again, they reasoned.

Wanda dressed her children in layers of clothing. One shirt was put on top of another with extra underwear. Romek and Danek each had two pairs of knickers with dark knee high socks and a dark jacket. "Why are we dressing this way? Why do we need so many clothes all at one time?" Romek asked.

"This way we don't have to pack a suitcase. Won't that be nice? No one will have to carry a heavy suitcase," Wanda replied. The children agreed. What an idea! No suitcases for this trip. Their bodies would be their suitcases. They were all thin, so the extra clothing did not make them look unusual.

The children continued dressing and giggling. All three children wore ankle-high leather shoes. Ela was dressed with one dress upon another with a thin white coat on top. All three children wore heavy stockings. Wanda wore a dress, a dark jacket, stockings, and whatever else could be worn and still look normal. The extra clothing actually felt good on the chilly morning. The summer was starting to change into fall and the evenings were becoming crisp. In the salt mine, it would also be cold.

The Wieliczka salt mines had existed since medieval times, over seven hundred years. Wanda had always wanted to take her children to see this unusual, creative wonder. From there it wasn't far to the Tatra Mountains. After the salt mine, she planned to take the children to the mountains and, from the top, cross into Czechoslovakia by foot.

Rumor had it that the mountaintop border separating Poland from Czechoslovakia was sparsely guarded. This seemed to be the easiest and safest way out of Poland. The trip, however, would be a hard one. Much of it would have to be on foot. From the top of the mountains, they would loop their way around into southern Germany, then travel up through the middle of the country into the British zone. It seemed like a good plan.

As always, before they left, they stood in a circle in front of the door, held each other, and prayed. They asked for safety, guidance, and God's blessing on this trip. After some final hugs and tears, they left.

Wanda sat quietly, without a word, as the train clacked along the tracks to Wieliczka. Thoughts were racing in her head. Was she doing the right thing? Would she ever see her mother, sisters, and Jagoda again? Was Józef really alive? Was he really in England? She had nothing in writing, just word-of-mouth information. Could it have been wrong? Should she change her plans? "Lord, please quiet my spirit. If this is what You want me to do, then let me feel at peace," she prayed.

The children were excited. They couldn't imagine what they were about to see. They had never gone into a mine. What a wonder to see carvings underground. They couldn't wait.

The train trip to Wieliczka was over almost before it started. They left the train and immediately went to the salt mine. Hundreds of steps led down deep into the belly of the salt mine. Wanda felt the chill of the clean underground air and saw the sculptures, the beautiful carved cathedral, the lakes–everything, but she was only going through the motions and "putting on a face" for her children. Her thoughts were continually on what was ahead and how to work out every detail.

From Wieliczka, it was only a short train ride to the mountains. From the edge of the mountain they took a trolley up as far as it would go. From there, they walked.

The mountainside looked incredibly peaceful—so different from how Wanda felt inside. A scattering of little cottages clung to the edge like tiny safe oases, beckoning. If only they could stay there at a more peaceful time. It would be a wonderful vacation spot.

As they approached the peak, the children raced ahead to see who could get there first. "Careful!" Wanda warned. Suddenly, Romek slipped and fell. His arm came crashing down against a sharp rock, cutting a deep wound into his arm. Romek looked at the wound but would not cry. He just sat there wincing as he watched the wound bleed. Wanda ran to her child. "Are you all right?"

"I'm all right, Mama." His voice quivered as he tried to sound brave. Looking at the wound, she wondered what she should do next. The wound definitely needed to be stitched, but where could she go? She took a bottle of water from her attaché case and poured it on the wound, then bandaged it tightly with a clean handkerchief and made a sling from her scarf.

They continued to the crest of the mountain where the border separated Poland from Czechoslovakia. But once there, they stood still. Just one more step, and they would be in Czechoslovakia. As predicted, no guards were at the boarder. A guardhouse was there and several people were there, but no guards.

As they stood on the mountaintop, ready to step over, Wanda felt very uneasy. *This is not the way to go*, she thought. *What if Romek's wound becomes infected? Where will I get help in these mountains? I really must get some ointment and a better bandage. Besides, my children can't speak Czech and we would be easily detected as foreigners.*

She walked over to a large rock and, in exasperation, sat down. Right there on the mountaintop she sat. What had she done? Had she gone this far for nothing? What should she do now? "Lord, I thought You were telling me to come up here. What am I supposed to do now?" she prayed.

As she prayed, an elderly couple approached her and started a conversation. There, on this mountaintop, she received word-of-mouth information that she accepted as truth. The couple told her that guides were available to help people cross the boarder at Görlitz, Poland. For a fee, they would carry people on their shoulders across the Nisse River into Germany. This was always done at night. They would meet their customers at an appointed place close to the river. Arrangements were made through these strangers that had quickly become friends.

Wanda could wait no longer. She had to tell her children. "Children, come here. Listen, this trip is more than a vacation. We are going to find Daddy and be with him. He is alive and lives far away in England." As she spoke, the children's eyes got wider and wider with amazement. This trip was getting more exciting all the time.

"When will we get there?" Danek asked.

"Probably not for a long time. We'll see," Wanda replied "We will have to be very careful not to tell anyone. Don't talk to anyone unless I tell you to and don't answer any questions."

"How will we get to England?" Romek asked as he cradled his arm.

"When we get to safety, we will send a telegram to Daddy and he will come and get us. Then we will take a big ship to England."

"But Mama, what about Grandma, Aunt Zosia, Aunt Czesia, and Jagoda?" Ela inquired. "I don't want to leave them."

"I know, dear, but we must find Daddy. When we get to safety, we will bring them to us."

The trolley ride back down the mountain was equally exciting, but for the children, whose minds were now filled with new information, questions loomed that would have to be answered later. Already they were practicing being silent.

At the base of the mountain, Wanda found a room for the night and purchased plenty of bandages and ointment for Romek's wound. In code, she sent a postcard to her mother and sisters: "Beloved Friends, We are enjoying our vacation in this beautiful place. Best wishes to all of you from Lonia."

Chapter 23

The Crossing

I am praying to you because I know you will answer, O God.
Bend down and listen as I pray. Show me your unfailing love
in wonderful ways. You save with your strength those who
seek refuge from their enemies.

—Psalm 17:6–7

Without a doubt, the mountains were beautiful beyond description—beautiful, majestic creations of God. Unfortunately, they
could not stay; they had to go on. A "safe house" on the outskirts
of Görlitz, Poland, would house Wanda and the children until
the day of their departure.

Secret arrangements were made and Wanda knew exactly
where and when she would meet the two guides who would
help them escape. People from the Underground made all the
arrangements. Several other contact addresses were given to her,
addresses of homes that would help as the family traveled. These
precious people helped at great risk to themselves. They helped
by providing shelter, offering food, and purchasing tickets. They
gave comfort to many displaced persons.

The day of the escape from Poland arrived. The sun was just
rising on that brisk September morning. Shiny enamel-covered

tin plates of food were placed in front of the children. Sleepily, they stared at the scrambled eggs. It was much too early to eat.

"Eat your breakfast. You'll need lots of energy today," Wanda told her three young children. "We'll be walking all day long and you need to be strong."

"Mama, when we prayed today, why did you cry?" seven-year-old Ela asked as she poked at her plate of eggs.

"It's because I'm so happy," Wanda answered, not wanting her children to know the real reason and not wanting them to be anxious. "Soon we will be with your daddy. We will be together again and you will have a much better life."

"But Mama," Danek broke in, looking at his mother, "You said it would be a long time before we see our daddy. He lives far away, in England." His logical, nine-year-old mind wanted to make sure that everything was clear.

The decision to leave Poland had not been easy to make. Through the Underground, Wanda had learned that her husband was alive and living in England. He had been captured as a prisoner of war, released through a miracle of God, and eventually joined the British army. She wondered if Józef knew that they were alive or where they had settled.

Passage to England could be arranged in the British Zone of West Germany, but only for immediate family members of British military personnel. In 1946 it was illegal to travel out of Poland without documents. The consequences could be fatal. How could she get through the heavily guarded borders? Then, how could she travel through Germany without documents?

"Will it be long before we cross the ocean on that huge ship?" her older son asked excitedly. Romek, in his ten years, had never seen a real ship, but his Aunt Zosia was a great storyteller. She often entertained the children with vivid descriptions of things she had seen and experienced.

"Sweetheart, only God knows that. We don't know how He will guide us. When we get to safety, we will write to Daddy. He will come and get us. It may be a very long time or perhaps not."

Not wanting to believe that it could be a long time, Romek excitedly plunged into his next sentence. "I can't wait! The ship will be so long that I know I won't be able to run from one end to the other without getting tired. I know! I'll be safe on the ship and no one will stop me."

"I'm going to eat ice cream all day long," Danek interjected. Such an incredible opportunity had never approached him before. "I know you can ask for more, anytime you want, and it won't cost anything."

"We're going to sleep way up high in the air on a bed that's on top of another bed." Romek stopped long enough to take a breath and raise another spoon of eggs to his thin face. "I'll explore the whole ship and the captain will let me go to the front and steer the ship."

"Don't talk with your mouth full. You'll choke!" Wanda admonished.

"He has a white uniform with gold buttons," Romek continued, ignoring his mother's advice. "Aunt Zosia told me. She said that she saw a captain once. I can't wait! We're going to have so much fun!"

Wanda looked away from the table as tears filled her eyes. Her young son's excitement pushed reality to the surface. The thought of parting from her precious mother, two sisters, and baby niece descended on her like a dark shroud. A heavy lump formed in her throat.

They had gone through so much together since World War II started. They had crossed war zones and dodged bombs. They hid from the enemy in ditches, in bombed-out buildings, in a cave, and in bomb shelters. They had prayed together and fasted together. After her little niece was born, Wanda and the others packed themselves into a cold cattle car and traveled in the middle of winter without heat, food, or drink. When they ran out of diapers, they all helped dry the diapers on their own bodies. They had suffered hunger together and thanked God for a crust of bread together. They had experienced more war than anyone should, and they were always together. How could they part now? If only they could all leave Poland together.

The days ahead were uncertain. Only God could know if they would survive and escape to freedom.

"Finish your breakfast, children. We need to leave very soon." Wanda's heart became unbearably heavy and full.

Quickly, she left the room and went outside behind the house to shed a few private tears and pray for strength and guidance. She lifted her eyes to heaven and said, "Only You know, dear God, if I shall ever see my mother and sisters again on this earth. Lord, I don't want to leave them, but I feel I must—for my children. I don't know what's ahead. I don't even know which direction to travel if we are able to cross the border. I'm so scared! Please give me courage for whatever is ahead. You have preserved us so many times before. I know you will be with us now. You are my God and I trust You."

For a few minutes she stayed there, leaning against the wall, remembering many things. She wanted to compose herself before she returned to her children. Remembering, she realized that in each dangerous situation, God was there. To have survived so many dangers and still be alive was indeed a miracle. With new courage, she returned to the children.

"It's time to get ready," she said.

The children were still dressed in layers of clothing; the same layers of clothing that they wore when they left Jabłonowo. There were no toys, no personal possessions, and no trinkets to take along on this trip. Although Romek was almost eleven, Danek nine, and Ela seven, they were still children. They were young, but almost didn't act as children. These were children of war. Every childish thing they had was left behind.

Their only luggage was a satchel that Wanda carried. It contained bread, dried fruit, a pretty scarf, a Bible, a package of cigarettes for barter, a few miscellaneous items, and a bottle of melted butter. Rumor had it that butter was very hard to get in Germany, so this could be a good barter item. For a moment Wanda wished she had her husband's prize possession, his camera. What a wonderful gift it would have been. That thought was only fleeting. Even if she did have the camera, if it had been found, they certainly would be charged with espionage. They could be interrogated, imprisoned, or even shot.

A wide river separated Poland from Germany. Wanda and the children would walk toward that border and hopefully arrive by dusk. Two guides, Jurek and Janusz, would meet them at the edge of the forest, take them to the border, and under cover of darkness, carry them across the river. These men were willing to risk their lives to save others—for a fee.

The walk to the border had begun. Wanda knew that the walk would be slow because her children would need time to rest. No form of transportation was available to where they were going. Walking through fields and along paths, they pretended to be just going for a leisurely walk.

By late afternoon, they were on the road that led to a village. Wanda had overheard that Russian troops were billeted in that village.

As they got closer, all of a sudden Russian soldiers approached with bayonets pointing directly at their bodies. Danek and Ela crowded tightly against their mother while Romek stood stiffly, almost as if paralyzed. The soldiers were suspicious of everyone, including children. Children were often used as spies by the Partisans and then rewarded with housing, extra food rations, or medical care. Partisans were men, like the Mafia, who spied on the Russians for the Underground. In the process, they would stalk and kill whoever got in their way.

"Where are you going?" the soldiers harshly demanded as they moved even closer.

Wanda tried to look calm and answered in a soft voice, "I am looking for my husband who is in the army. He is stationed somewhere near here. My children haven't seen their father for a long time and they miss him." Her heart was pounding so hard that it felt as if it would jump out of her body. "I'd like to visit with him for a little while, but I'm afraid of the Partisans."

Slowly, the soldiers lowered their bayonets and said, "Don't be afraid. Just follow this road; it will lead you right to the village. I'm sure you will find him there."

Wanda thanked them and, holding her breath, started to walk away, praying that they would not ask her any more questions. Wanda and the children did their best to act as if they belonged, as if they really were walking toward the village. When the soldiers were out of sight, they quickly ran into the dense forest and hid among the trees.

Quietly, they stopped and listened, waiting for any repercussion. When they felt it was safe, they slowly inched their way though the forest. Every step had to be calculated. No stepping on twigs that may snap. They walked as if on air, hardly making a sound.

The forest stood next to a strip of land that was called "no man's land." Tall wild grasses covered the ground next to the river that divided Poland from East Germany. Trained dogs were guarding the area and listening devices were everywhere. The Russians could hear if anyone was around and trying to escape.

By twilight, Wanda and the children were at the edge of the forest where they would meet the guides, Jurek and Janusz.

As they quietly waited, she whispered some final instructions. "I know it will be hard, but remember, absolutely *no* talking.

Our lives depend on it. You will have to be quiet for a long, long time. I will let you know when you can speak again." She gave them each a little hug, then put her finger across her lips as a reminder.

It was evening when the guides arrived. Wanda had never met the men and still had an edge of fear. Were these really guides? Were they truly here to help? She had to trust someone. She had asked God for guidance. She did trust Him.

Both guides were dressed in dark clothing. Their faces blended into the shadows. Janusz was muscular and the taller of the two. Jurek was a little shorter and stocky, but also looked strong.

The sun had set but the moon was out and it was much too light to cross. How could they move about and not be seen? The children started to get a little restless. Wanda was concerned about how long they could wait quietly and not be heard or seen.

"Dear Lord", she prayed, "we're here, but the moon is so bright. How can we cross safely? You have watched over us and protected us more times than I can count. Please show us Your mercy again. Please, I pray, surround us with fog to hide us from our enemies."

Wanda did not have to wait for an answer to her prayer. Opening her eyes, she watched in awe as a heavy fog started to form in the empty field before them. This was no ordinary fog. It was big balls of fog.

As if spellbound, the guides also looked at the fog forming around them. "We have never seen anything like this!" Jurek whispered with wonder in his voice. "Tonight, in this fog, we could take a hundred people across."

Wanda felt goose bumps all over her body. Never did she expect an answer so quickly and so completely. Shivers went up and down her spine as the fog thickened.

Truly God is with us, she thought. *If anyone* ever *didn't believe in God, they certainly would tonight; they would know that God answers prayers.* There was no explanation for this fog except that it was a gift from God. Wanda accepted it humbly and gratefully.

Without hesitation they all walked, surrounded by this fog. Single file, they walked along the bank of the deep river. They walked till they came to a sharp bend in the river. There, they stopped.

Years ago, big flat rocks and boulders were placed several feet beneath the water to stop the erosion. The guides knew about these rocks and knew exactly where they were placed.

As they prepared to cross, searchlights swept the field on the East German side of the river. Quietly, the family sat beside a small clump of shrubbery while the men removed their shoes and outer clothing, and hid them.

Everything was quiet except for the rushing waters. Everyone listened for rustling or soldiers' voices. All was quiet. Not even the bark of a dog was heard. Jurek looked at the children with their ghost-white, anxious faces and smiled. With his smile and a nod of the head, he told them that everything would be all right.

Jurek quickly motioned to Danek. Danek knew what was next. The courageous, slight boy quickly walked to the stranger, who immediately lifted him onto his shoulders and grasped his hands firmly in his. Danek was small for his age, but brave to the core. He gritted his teeth, closed his long lashed eyes, and just hung on. He didn't even look back as they walked toward the cold, dark water.

Romek was next. Janusz eased him onto his strong shoulders and both started toward the foreboding waters. Hesitating, he looked back at his mother. She nodded her head in approval and motioned for them to go.

Slowly, the entourage entered the water and disappeared in the fog. At first the water level was just to their thighs. Quickly it rose to the guides' chests. Slowly, they felt their way across the slippery rocks, shivering in the cold water.

The current of the river was strong and it took a lot of strength to keep their balance. Before long, they were on the other shore. The guides lifted the boys onto the bank. Romek and Danek hunched down low and watched as the guides disappeared back into the dark water. The brothers were alone—on the other side of the wide river.

Wanda and Ela stared intently into the fog, waiting for the guides to return. Somehow it took longer than Wanda had expected.

Are the boys all right? Will they remember not to talk? Could they have slipped and fallen into the water? Did the river carry them away? Her anxious thoughts ran rampant. The wait was excruciating! *Where were the guides?*

All of a sudden, in the darkness, she heard rustling. She looked around, didn't see anything, and then listened again. Her heart pounded in her ears, almost drowning out the sounds of the river. It was difficult to tell at first where the rustling came from. She looked around, then breathed a sigh of relief as she saw Jurek approaching. Janusz came close behind. They had returned at a different spot, not where Wanda had expected.

Without a word, Jurek took Ela, placed her on his shoulders, and started to walk toward the water.

Janusz, the stronger and taller of the two, motioned for Wanda to follow him. Stepping into the water, he pointed to a huge boulder on the bank. In silence, he pantomimed for her to get onto the rock and climb on his shoulders. She did not hesitate. Quickly she climbed onto the damp, slippery rock and promptly slipped and fell, scraping her knees and nearly dropping her precious satchel into the water. She lay there only a moment before regaining her composure. Gingerly, she stood and eased herself onto Janusz's strong shoulders.

Would he be strong enough to carry her and fight the current? Janusz took her hands in his, balancing her along with her satchel, and walked into the river.

It was only a moment before Wanda could feel the cold water as it rushed into her shoes and soaked her stockings. She could not see Jurek and Ela and wondered if they were safely across.

The water rose higher and higher on Janusz's chest as he carried Wanda through the river. Trying to keep her dress dry, she gathered up the material from her skirt and pulled it up over her head. Silently, the guide jerked his shoulders, telling her to keep still. They could both end up underwater.

Trying to stay dry was useless. The river got deeper and deeper, and soon Wanda was partially submerged in the cold water.

When everyone was safely delivered to the west side of the river, the guides slipped quietly into the water and were gone.

The little family was now alone. The fog was lifting and was not as dense as before. Searchlights arched on the west side of the river, washing the field with their bright lights. There were no trees or bushes to hide behind. How were they going to cross this field?

Wanda lay down on the ground next to her children to catch her breath. The grass was wet and slippery from the evening dew.

"Dear God," she prayed, "the searchlights can still see us through this fog. Please close the eyes of the guards so that we can cross this field safely."

Lovingly, she looked at her children, wondering what would be next. The children, silently, trustingly, looked back at their mother. Romek, Danek, and Ela quietly put their heads down on the ground beside her, waiting for the next cue.

The cool evening and the wet clothing chilled Wanda's body. It was then that she realized how tired she was. She rested a moment, listening to the sound of the rushing river, wishing she could give in to her exhaustion. But this was not the time to rest.

"Watch me carefully," she whispered, her voice camouflaged by the sound of the river. "We will hold hands and run together," she instructed. "When the searchlights start to come in our direction, we will quickly lay down flat on the ground and be very, very still until the light is gone again. Just remember, we still can't talk–at all."

As she lifted her head, she realized that Ela had a light colored coat and she would be very visible. Quickly, she took off her dark jacket and placed it on her child. The jacket hung loosely and the sleeves hung over her hands. Hurriedly, she rolled up the sleeves, exposing her small hands.

Wanda held Ela's hand tightly in her own and with the other hand held the satchel and Danek's hand. Romek held on to his brother.

"Are we ready?" she whispered as they all crouched down.

When the time was right, she jumped up and ran with the children. The children's legs didn't move as fast as she had hoped. If only she could hold them all in her arms, she could get them across the field faster.

They ran until the searchlights approached, then quickly laid down on the ground. Over and over they followed this pattern. The children knew that this wasn't a game and that what was happening was very serious and important to all of them. Slowly, at a little girl's pace, they made their way across the wide field.

Out of the range of the searchlights and having reached the safety of the other side of the field, they started to walk toward the town.

The cool night air brushed against their cold cheeks and Wanda, still dressed in wet clothing, shivered.

"Mama, I'm so tired. Are we almost there?" Ela whispered as they continued walking toward the town.

On the outskirts of this town was an apple orchard. Through it they could see the streets and houses. It was late and nearly all the residents were asleep. The few lights in the windows invited them near. The oil lamps cast gentle beams through the windows onto the neighborhood.

Wanda had received an address to a "safe house" within the town. She was confident that they would shelter them for the night with no questions asked. She was told to throw a pebble at the upstairs window and someone would let them in.

As her eyes adjusted to the new light, Wanda was able to make out some of the street signs and numbers. Cautiously, she walked down the street, looking and listening for anyone who might be following. A curfew was in effect, and no one was to be out. The night was still and quiet. No one was in sight. Searching anxiously, she located the house.

"Romek, help me find a little stone!" she whispered to her oldest son. Romek was very tired, but did his best to stay alert. Her two younger children were fading from exhaustion.

Romek, sensing her anxiety, and with wisdom beyond his years said, "Everything will be all right, Mama. God will take care of us." He hunched down by the edge of the street and felt for a small pebble. "Is this the right size, Mama?" he whispered.

"That's good, find some more." Wanda looked at the two-story house as Romek searched for more stones. She had been told to throw a pebble at the window on the second floor—but which window? She aimed carefully at the window above the front door. She missed. She tried again. This time the tiny pebble reached its mark. Nothing happened. She tried again. Again, nothing happened.

Oh, God, what shall we do if no one answers? Fear crept over her as she thought of the possibilities. Was this the wrong address? What should she do? They were traveling in a foreign country, illegally, without papers and without knowing anyone there. Where should they go now?

Wanda took another pebble and just as she threw it at the window, the front door opened. In the darkness, she could not see the face of the person who stood in the doorway. A hand motioned for them to come in and then disappeared into the darkness. Hesitating for just a moment, Wanda gave the children a gentle push. The children led the way into the darkened room.

After the door was closed behind them the figure spoke in the darkness.

"I'm sorry, I don't have any beds or blankets to offer you, but if you want to rest on the floor, at least you'll be safe."

Without blankets or pillows, or any fanfare, the exhausted family lay down directly on the wooden floor.

Never did floorboards make such a wonderful, comforting bed. They now felt safe and warm. The exhausted children tucked their coats under their heads and, pushing up against each other, immediately fell asleep.

Wanda's head was reeling from the events of the day. She could not sleep. She prayed into the night, thanking God for the miracles of the day and asking for strength and a clear mind for tomorrow.

What would tomorrow bring? Soon exhaustion overcame her and she too fell asleep.

Chapter 24

Unbelievable Kindness

O Lord, I have come to you for protection; don't let me be put to shame. Rescue me, for you always do what is right.

Bend down and listen to me; rescue me quickly. Be for me a great rock of safety, a fortress where my enemies cannot reach me.

—Psalm 31:1–2

The morning glow started to outline the rooftops on another crisp September morning. Everything was quiet on the street of this post-war East German town. By all impressions, everything looked ordinary. Who would have guessed that a mother and her three young children, sleeping on the floor in the front hall of this ordinary house, on this ordinary street, had just lived through an extraordinary experience, through an experience that only God could have arranged and orchestrated?

Hours before, they had crossed a heavily guarded river border and walked through the night street patrolled by soldiers. Searchlights, dogs, listening devices, and armed soldiers could not hinder God's hand. He heard and answered the sincere prayer of a woman who loved Him and depended on Him explicitly.

Although Wanda and the children were still in a dangerous situation, they were closer to freedom.

At dawn, the household stirred. Wanda immediately woke and rose as the children continued sleeping, still cuddled close to each other. The lack of a pillow or blanket didn't disturb them.

"I'm so sorry that I didn't have extra bedding for you last night," Mrs. Volkmann said as she approached Wanda. "I hope you got some rest," the gentle homeowner spoke in hushed tones as she entered the hallway. "I had to lend my extra bedding to someone yesterday. I didn't know that we would have visitors."

"We slept very well, thank you," Wanda replied. "Thank you for your kindness. Thank you for opening your home to us. Look at the children. They are sleeping as if at home in their own beds."

"I'll prepare breakfast. Please join my husband and me at the table and we will discuss the plans for today. You will need to have an early start," she spoke, soothing Wanda with her voice.

Still exhausted, Wanda woke the children and started getting them ready for the day.

Over a wonderful breakfast of bread, sliced tomato, and tea, they discussed the plans for the day. Mr. Volkmann started and spoke in a solid, low tone, "We will buy train tickets for you to Annaberg, which is south from here. It's in the mountains, close to the Czechoslovakian border."

"But I need to go north to the British zone," Wanda protested.

"If you travel north from here, your documents will be continually scrutinized. That could be a problem, since you have no documents. If you travel north from southern Germany, Annaberg, you may have a better chance; they will not be checking them as closely. We have found this to be a good diversionary tactic." He paused. "When you arrive in Annaberg, go to Mr. and Mrs. Sheffer's home. They will take you in and take good care of you. Memorize their address. They are good people. You'll be safe there." He lowered his glasses, rubbed his face, and continued. "The train leaves early this morning so we don't have a lot of time. Oh, by the way, you will need to transfer in Dresden."

Wanda retrieved money from her clothing and handed it to Mr. Volkmann. It was impossible for Poles to purchase tickets in East Germany. Quickly, he left, exchanged the Polish zloty for German marks, bought the tickets, and returned home.

While the sun was still rising and casting long shadows on the neighborhood, Wanda and the children hastily walked to the station. Rays of sunshine filtered through the trees and landed in patches on the streets, giving the day a fresh start and planting new hope in Wanda's heart.

"When we get on the train, don't speak, be very quiet," Wanda cautioned her children as they approached the station. "If the conductor is near, be sure your eyes are closed so that he will think you are sleeping. That way, he won't ask you any questions."

The train was crowded, but seats were found for the children. Leaving them alone, Wanda dodged around the train, avoiding the conductor. Tickets were one thing, but traveling without permission, without documents, was a severe violation of the law. When the conductor was at the front of the train, she slid to the back. When he came close, she ducked into the lavatory, then out of the lavatory, milled with the passengers, and watched her children from a distance. Her eyes were always looking all around suspiciously, looking for danger, but yet, she had to look inconspicuous. It helped that she had no luggage, just her satchel containing her precious Polish Bible. If this was discovered, this alone could have caused her a lot of distress. During the escape there was no time to read the Bible, but just knowing that it was in her satchel gave her comfort.

Arriving in Dresden, memories of the previous year flooded into Wanda's being. The ruins, the straw, the dead, the pistol, the drunk soldier, the abduction at gunpoint, hiding in the ruins all night, Anna calling her, Zosia huddled in a dark boxcar, the children crying. Everything came spinning back to her. And this all happened *after* the war ended. The horror of it all made her shiver.

Quickly, they disembarked and looked for the transfer train. The sooner she was off the platform, the safer she felt. Again, she instructed the children, "Sit very quietly, sleep whenever the conductor is near, and remember, don't speak Polish!"

The train started. Again, she shuffled from car to car, avoiding the conductor. As the hours passed, when she felt it was safe, she sat by her children. When they started to wake from their sleep, she pinched their thighs as a reminder not to speak Polish. Adrenaline kept her alert even though they traveled deep into the night.

At three A.M., the train arrived in Annaberg. What months of memories remained there: God's amazing hand as He guided her family out of Dresden just hours before it became an inferno, the wonderful provision of food and shelter, protection during air raids and bombings, healing Danek's illness, and Zosia's broken leg. *God is so good*, she thought.

As they stepped onto the platform, Wanda knew exactly where to go. She was familiar with the streets. Arriving at the Sheffers' address, she threw a stone at a window. Before long, the upstairs window opened and a whispering voice asked, "Who is it?"

"Mrs. Volkmann," Wanda responded, not using her own name because it wouldn't be recognized.

"I'll be right down," the voice answered.

"Come in, come in," she quickly invited. "What? You're not Mrs. Volkmann!" Mrs. Sheffer remarked.

"Mr. and Mrs. Volkmann sent us and said you would give us shelter," Wanda whispered.

"Of course, come in. Of course you're welcome," she said as she lit a small kerosene lamp. "Oh, bless you. Look at these precious children. You must all be exhausted. Are you hungry? Of course you are. Come into the kitchen. After you have something to eat and drink, you can sleep. Come," she beckoned. They followed the light into the kitchen and sat around the big oval table. "Here, here's some bread, jam, and milk. This will help you sleep and hold you till morning," she said as she poured the room temperature milk into cups. Before eating, as always, Wanda and the children thanked God for the food and for these wonderful people and their home.

As they ate, a sleepy Mr. Sheffer stumbled down the stairs wrapped in a coat, with long underwear protruding from beneath it. "Good morning, friends. Oh, we have children tonight! We're glad you arrived safely."

Wanda and the children had no idea what generosity lay ahead. When they had finished eating, Mr. and Mrs. Sheffer ushered them upstairs to their very own bedroom. Wanda looked at the room and exclaimed, "But this is your room!" It was simply furnished, but wonder of wonders, the bed was outfitted with a featherbed.

"We know! We want you to have it tonight. Sleep as long as you want. When you wake, we will make plans for the next part of your journey. God bless you. Sleep well," she said as she closed the door.

Wanda and the children stood there hardly knowing what to do next. Here they were, exhausted and dirty. For days they had worn the same clothing, the same layers of clothing. They had wandered through the salt mines, trekked up and down the mountains, journeyed through the deep river, laid on the damp ground, and slept on the floor, all without washing or even changing their clothes and now they had been invited to sleep in this wonderful, clean featherbed…without taking a bath? Yes, they were all exhausted and it was almost morning, but into this warm, clean bed without a bath? It was inconceivable. Where did these incredible, generous people come from? *Were they angels?* Wanda wondered.

Without any more thought, Wanda helped the children undress and quickly got them all into bed. They laid down like sardines in a can, two heads at one end and two at the other.

"Dear Lord, how can these dear people allow us, strangers, to sleep in their marvelous bed? Lord, I know You will reward them in heaven, but please bless them even now while here on earth," she prayed. "Sometimes I just wonder if I can go on. Lord, I know You're with me but honestly, I'm really weary of all this stress and anxiety. How long can we dodge the soldiers, the rifles, and horror? If we are to die, then please let us die right here in this wonderful warm place. This bed feels like no other, like a cloud. If we are to die, then please let us die right here." She snuggled deep under the feathers and quickly fell asleep.

Most of the morning was gone by the time Wanda awoke. She allowed the children to continue sleeping as she dressed and went downstairs.

Mr. and Mrs. Sheffer greeted her warmly and invited her to sit. They shared their food and drink as plans were made for the next part of the journey.

"Our hearts are really touched by your courage. Traveling with children is not easy. It's been a long time since we've had children in this home. We had two grown sons, but they're gone now." Mrs. Sheffer said as her eyes welled up with tears. "We miss them so much." Wanda did not ask what happened. She knew.

"This morning I bought tickets for you and the children to Göttingen," Mr. Sheffer informed. "That's where you will cross into the British zone."

"Thank you. You are very kind. How much do I owe you?" Wanda retrieved the currency hidden in her clothes and handed it to him. She had money hidden on her person. Because she dressed simply and did not look as though she had money, no one bothered her and did not steal from her.

"Could you spare a loaf of bread for our journey?"

"Of course, of course. Here, take it." Wanda took the bread, and tried to pay Mrs. Sheffer but she wouldn't accept the money.

"I am so grateful for all you have done. Please take it," Wanda pleaded.

"No, we really can't. It is our pleasure. It's for the children, they will need it," the gracious lady replied.

How could she express her heartfelt gratitude to these wonderful people? Wanda opened her briefcase and removed her beautiful scarf. Lovingly, she unfolded it and placed it around Mrs. Sheffer's neck. As tears flowed, Wanda said, "I can never thank you enough for your kindness. God be with both of you and God bless you."

Observing this exchange, Mr. Sheffer sniffled and said, "Mother, we won't be traveling any time soon. Why don't you lend your traveling documents to Wanda? She may need them. She can mail them back to us from the British zone."

It was hard to leave these wonderful, generous people, but leave they must. After a few rounds of hugs and kisses, they walked to the station.

This train was a regular passenger train with several compartments in each car. Doors were placed strategically at each end of each compartment, one door opened to the platform, the other to the inside hall. Seats were stretched across from each other with luggage racks overhead. The hallway ran the length of each car with a lavatory at the end.

The train was jammed, incredibly packed with people. Masses of people still waited on the platform, pushing, trying to inch their way onto the train. And so were Wanda and her children. It was impossible to enter through the door. "We have to get on! We have tickets for this train. We have to keep going. Lord, help me!" she cried.

Wanda looked up and saw an open window, a window to the lavatory. "Quickly, come here!" she motioned to her children. "Quick, I'll boost you up through the window." She grabbed Danek and the spry boy was inside in a wink.

The train whistle blew loud and clear. It was ready to depart. Romek followed through the window, but needed extra help.

Slowly, the train started to move. Once Romek was inside, she threw her satchel through the open window and anxiously called to her sons, "Grab Ela, quick!" Ela stretched her arms toward her brothers as Wanda raised her up. They reached and pulled her inside.

The engine hissed as it started to move away from the station. The children watched in horror as Wanda ran alongside the train, dodging past the people, trying to jump and grab hold of the edge of the window frame. Could she make it in time? Was she strong enough? What if they were separated? What would the children do without their mother? "Jesus, help me!" she pleaded.

One more jump and she caught hold of the frame. She hung by her fingertips as the train approached the end of the platform. Strength failed her as she tried to pull herself up. "Come on, Mama, come on. Try again," the children implored. She hung there, limp.

Out of nowhere, strong hands appeared and boosted her up, pushing her through the window. By the time she struggled in, turned around, and leaned out the window, no one was in sight.

For a few moments, the family stayed packed into the tiny space and took in what had just happened. The children were all on the verge of tears as Wanda trembled and tried to compose herself. "We can't stay in here." The lavatory was tiny and smelled putrid. "Remember what I told you before, don't speak Polish." They opened the door and squeezed their way into the cabin.

The train compartments were so crowded that it was almost impossible to breathe. Ela held her mother's hand tightly and felt as if she would be crushed. As the train made its stops, passengers got off and made room for others. It was a difficult trip.

A person sitting at a window seat saw Wanda and her children and offered it to them. All four squeezed into the one seat with Ela on Wanda's lap. They all proceeded to pretend to fall asleep.

When she heard the conductor approaching, she quickly left the children and went to the opposite end of the train. Like a detective, she moved from here to there, from there to here, spying, but trying not to be seen by the conductor.

The conductor did not catch her so he did not ask for her papers, the borrowed papers that did not even match her description. The children pretended to be in a deep sleep and the conductor did not question them.

The rhythmic clatter of the tracks soothed Danek and he did fall into a deep sleep. Wanda returned to the compartment and sat beside him. As he was waking, he forgot where he was and, speaking loudly in Polish, he blurted, "I knew we were riding on a train." Wanda's heart stopped! Frightened, she looked around to see who was watching and who heard him. From then on she paid even closer attention to her children and was ready to pinch their thighs whenever they weren't alert. And so the trip continued day and night.

The children could not behave as normal children. They were taught to keep quiet and not trust anyone. They could not respond to normal instincts. Talking, laughing, or even loud breathing was not allowed. They had to be invisible. During that time, there was no playtime or fun. Before speaking, they had to think carefully. Should they answer? What language should they speak? They also could not use the bathroom just any time they needed to. They lived in constant fear. Many tears and screams were pent up inside their beings, possibly never to be released.

"Mama, do we have any bread?" Ela whispered in her mother's ear as she watched the woman across from her. In one hand, the woman held a bright, shiny, red tomato and in the other, a crust of dry black bread. Ela looked longingly at the tomato and bread. The bread from Annaberg was already gone. Nothing was left, not even a dry crust. The children were hungry. They were always hungry.

As before, Wanda did not eat so that her children could have food. When no drink was available, not even water or tea, she drank beer and gave the children beer to drink. It was inexpensive and there were no other choices.

"When we transfer in Halle we'll see if we can buy something," Wanda whispered.

During the night, the train stopped in Halle, East Germany. This is where they had an overnight stopover. As hard as they looked, no food or drink could be bought, only beer. There was no clean water, no milk, no tea, and no food. As they walked a little farther, at last, a lonely vender was selling soup.

"What kind of soup are you selling?" Wanda asked as she looked at the horrible black mixture in the pot.

"It's vegetable soup," the vendor replied. The soup was inexpensive, just pennies. Since there was no other choice, Wanda bought four small bowls.

The vendor took previously used soup bowls, dipped them in a bucket of dirty water, and ladled the soup into the bowls. Ela, Romek, and Danek eagerly ate the soup. Then the vendor gave Wanda her bowl. Hoping that the soup tasted better than it looked, the starving mother lifted it to her lips. She paused. It smelled terrible. She took a sip, but could not swallow it. It sickened her. It tasted even worse than she had imagined. The mixture was made of dried cabbage and dried potatoes and who knew what else. It had no meat, no fat, and not even a little salt to flavor it. She gave it to her hungry children, who ate it without complaining. When the soup was gone, the bowls were returned to the vendor to be used again by some starving person.

A corner of the *bahnhof* (station) was found where they could settle down for the night. Wanda sat down on the concrete while Ela leaned up against her. Romek and Danek promptly stretched out and tucked their arms under their heads.

Morning would soon arrive, along with the train to Göttingen. In Göttingen they would attempt to cross the border between East and West Germany.

Chapter 25

Tree of Safety

But those who wait on the Lord will find new strength. They will fly high on wings like eagles. They will run and not grow weary. They will walk and not faint.

—Isaiah 40:31

Around five o'clock in the afternoon of the next day, the train arrived in Göttingen. The overcast sky reflected the mood of the children. The pinching, prodding, shuffling, and hiding made the children continually tense but alert.

"No talking, no questions, and no misbehaving as we go to the border. Whatever happens, just try to blend in," Wanda cautioned again. "Once we cross this border, we will be in the British zone of Germany and then we will be safe and can all relax. I know this has been hard for you, but it's almost over."

The silent walk to the border took about twenty minutes. They were almost there. On both sides of the road were woods. Wanda edged the children into the woods and there whispered some final instructions, "You stay here and I'll walk alone to the border." She felt that if she needed to run, then the children would have a head start.

"Watch me carefully, but don't let them see you," she cautioned. "I'll talk to the crossing guard. If he lets us cross, I'll wave and you come quickly. Do you all understand? This is very important." Romek and Danek, with eyes round as saucers, shook their heads in the affirmative.

"One more thing. If I start to run, you run into the woods and hide. I'll find you later." For a moment, she held her children, sent a silent prayer to heaven, and to her children said, "Don't worry, God will take care of us."

In the distance she could see the guardhouse where the Russian soldiers gathered. Talking and music came from the house. She watched a little longer till only one guard was at the gate.

"I'll be watching you from a distance, and you watch me," she repeated in a whisper as she started walking toward the border alone.

I must relax. I have to look calm. Lord, help me say the right words. Please quiet my spirit, Lord Jesus, she prayed as her heart pounded against her ribs. She knew that without documents, it was very dangerous or even impossible to cross the border, but she believed in miracles.

With a pleasant expression on her face, she cautiously approached the border guard and prepared to negotiate.

She started out with some small talk. "What a day! It looks like rain."

He perked up and said, "Yes, I felt a few drops earlier." He was glad to have the opportunity to talk to a pretty lady.

"May I ask you something?" she asked.

"What is it?"

"My husband is across the border and I would like to go and visit him for a little while. Do you know how I could arrange that?"

As she spoke, she kept an eye on her children standing in the distance.

"Oh, you have a husband?"

"Yes, and I have children. I really would appreciate some information. They haven't seen their father for a long time. I thought a little visit would perk them up."

He looked at the ground as his shoe traced a rut in the soil.

"I don't have much to offer, but I do have a package of cigarettes for whoever can give me that information."

He casually looked at the guardhouse and said, "When it's dinner time, in about half an hour, try crossing through the woods, over there." With his eyes he indicated the direction. He did not dare point, in case his comrades were watching.

"Fewer soldiers will be guarding the area during dinner. Perhaps you will have success." He paused. "On the other side of the woods is a wide field. When you reach the huge fallen tree in the field, you will be at the border." Then nonchalantly he said, "Leave the cigarettes by that tree past the guard house." Again, pointing with his eyes.

Wanda thanked him and casually walked toward the tree he indicated. Stooping as if to fix her shoe, she placed the cigarettes by the tree. Calmly, she walked down the road to the edge of the woods where her children were hiding.

As they waited in the woods, the rain started to fall. First it was gentle, and then it turned into a hard, torrential rain. Soldiers ran to the shelter from all directions. They left the areas that they were patrolling. But some may have stayed at their posts, Wanda reasoned.

It was time, the exact time to walk where the border guard indicated. "Step carefully," Wanda cautioned. "Don't break any twigs, rustle the leaves, or make noise." Quickly, they walked through the woods.

Along the way, remnants of people's lives were strewn everywhere. This apparently had been a way of escape for others. Suitcases that had become too heavy to carry were left abandoned. Most of them were broken open and rifled through, spilling clothes and photographs into a jumble of trash. The most precious possession became so much excess baggage when life was at stake. Only God knew if the owners of these suitcases survived.

They continued walking through the woods with the blessing of God covering them in a torrential rain. This rain protected them from the soldiers that were ordered to shoot anyone attempting to cross the border.

As they approached the edge of the woods, they faced the large grassy field. There, in the distance, lay the huge fallen tree. There it rested in majesty, offering its life as a goal post for those racing to survive, those reaching for a better life.

But now the rain was letting up and, with that, the soldiers would soon come back again. She still had to take the children across the wide field. Quickly they started but were only part way across when they heard a heavy rumbling of motorcycles in the distance. Where could they hide?

Close by stood a dilapidated shed. Quickly, they dashed into the shed and hid under the broken window at the front of the shed. *Are they looking for us? Did the guard give us away?* As she wondered, the motorcycles came closer and closer, slowed down, and then went right past the shed, across the field, and out of sight.

When they were gone, Wanda quickly led the children across the field. It was now or never. It was still light but there was no recourse. Farther and farther across the field they rushed till they reached the tree, the precious tree of safety. They were now in the British Zone of Germany. Safe!

From there it was only a short walk to the town and the address that the dear people in Annaberg gave. Here was food and shelter. After offering them a good night's sleep, the kind people purchased tickets to Hamburg and gave Wanda an address for the next stop. They were still traveling without documents, which could cause problems, but they were no longer in such terrible danger as before.

The stopover in Hamburg was memorable. On September 25, 1946, Romek turned eleven. The celebration was wonderful. There were no gifts and no cake, but there were wonderful fried potatoes with onions and a tasty dark soup made from rye flour. No horrible black soup. What a feast! What a celebration for all of them.

These wonderful Christian strangers who provided this extraordinary celebration also gave them comfortable overnight accommodations. The next day, they took them to a German Christian agency that cared for displaced people.

The agency provided information, money, and shelter till arrangements could be made for the final stop in Germany, the displaced people's camp in Eckernförde. Once there, Wanda would try to contact Józef. Hopefully all this effort, all this danger, was not in vain. Was Józef really alive? Was he really in England? Wanda hoped and prayed that it was true. From there she planned to send a telegram to England–and wait.

Chapter 26

Safe at Last

Not to us, O Lord, but to you goes all the glory for your unfailing love and faithfulness.

—Psalm 115:1

I look up to the mountain – does my help come from there? My help comes from the Lord, who made the heavens and the earth!

—Psalm 121:1–2

At last, Wanda and her children arrived in Eckernförde, the destination that spelled freedom, a new start, and a start toward a better life, a life with Wanda's husband, Józef. It spelled, HOPE. It all stemmed on the hope that what she heard was the truth and that Józef was really in England.

Holding her breath, she still couldn't help but wonder, *What if Józef was not in England? What if fleeing Poland brought them to another dead end? Would the British let them stay or would they have to return?*

Eckernförde was a camp for displaced people run by the British army. It was designed and built under Hitler's direction and patterned after his extermination camps. But now it housed those who had nowhere else to go. It was not intended to be permanent housing, but only temporary until something better could be arranged.

Wanda and the children stood in the camp looking like lost sheep, exhausted, dirty, and dazed. The corridors of buildings all looked alike. Where should they go? The compound did not look welcoming. Rows and rows of buildings lined the street but there were no trees, flowers, or living things to decorate the complex.

Entering the first building, they stood in one large room the length of the building. It was shockingly furnished. Chairs surrounded a single table and a long row of connected bunk-bed-type beds lined the entire length of the long wall. But what curious beds! They looked like double-decked platforms with a scattering of straw on top. Each bed could accommodate a whole family.

Although the surroundings were drab, the atmosphere inside was welcoming. Children sat around the table, talking, laughing, and eating smoked fish heads. As they sucked on the fish brains, they invited Wanda's children. "Come join us, they're good." The three children just watched as Wanda received instructions where she should go to be registered.

Registration and what followed was an incredible experience. First there was a medical exam and a lice check, then temporary housing was assigned and food ration cards were given. As if this wasn't enough, a floodgate of generosity was opened. Through the kindness of strangers, wonderful things were given to the family. First came an invitation to a meal, then came sheets, blankets, pillows, and washing supplies. It was more than they could hold in their arms. They had help moving everything to their new dwelling.

Next came an invitation to rummage through the UNRA (United Nations Relief Association) boxes. What an exciting privilege! The boxes were massive—large enough to house all three children. With the children's help, Wanda picked out a set of clothing for each of them, which included warm winter coats, hats, gloves, and shoes.

Several smaller sealed boxes were then presented, which they took to their sleeping quarters. Upon opening them, incredible abundance poured out: powdered milk, tea, powdered eggs, and dried cheese, along with other necessities. Two other items were in this box that made the children feel as if it were Christmas: concentrated orange juice in a bottle (an unheard of treat) and *chocolate!* The children could hardly believe it. They could not remember the last time they had had chocolate.

The following day, Wanda set about confirming what she had heard through the Underground. The office proceeded checking. Now, new thoughts muddled her mind. What if Józef was alive but lost hope that his family was still alive? What if he found someone else and got married again? He was extremely handsome and a very desirable man. She had to chase those thoughts away.

She got busy and occupied her mind with other things. The traveling documents had to be mailed back to the Sheffers. She added some of her new food ration cards as a thank-you.

A letter had to be written, in code, to her mother and sisters. What a joy to be able to send good news.

The sooner everyone got into a schedule, the better. The boys were registered at a temporary school.

Ela, at seven years old, attended school in Jabłonowo, but only for a few weeks before they left. Here she attended an activities center with other children her age. There she had her first experience with colored pencils. Drawing became her passion. Curiously, she always started her pictures from the bottom of the page. Feet and shoes appeared first, then a skirt, shoulders, arms, and, last of all, the head. Adults enjoyed watching the pictures emerge.

Wanda found part-time work in the kitchen. It brought in a little money and made her feel useful. Her character would not allow her to waste time.

Within a few days, Wanda was ecstatic. Good news had arrived. Józef was alive! He was indeed alive! Alive and well! He had defected from the German army and joined the British forces. He was alive and well and living in England! Wanda was elated! She could hardly contain herself. It was amazing to see that word of mouth information could travel so accurately through the Underground.

Józef still did not know that his family was among the living. How could he know where to even start searching for them? So much of Poland had been bombed, so many people had died, and nearly everyone was displaced from their homes.

Wanda immediately sent a telegram to England, informing him that they were all alive and safe in Eckernförde.

In short order, a telegram came back informing Wanda that he would immediately start the process to acquire visas for the family. He would come to get them as soon as possible.

Within a few weeks, new housing became available for Wanda and the children. A little two-room cottage, snuggled in a pine forest, would be shared with a lovely older man and his wife. It was comfortable, but very small. The rooms were just large enough to contain two small beds, a small table that fit perfectly between the beds, and a chair. Separating the two rooms was a kitchen just large enough in which to turn around. Yes, it was small, but wonderful and, at last, private. They could close the door and be alone as a family.

Along with the new accommodations came new supplies: a nestling set of aluminum cooking pots, a mixing bowl, large cooking spoons, plates, cups, and silverware.

Romek immediately wanted to get involved and make a special treat for his whole family. He got a big pot of water, set it on the stove, and said, "It's going to be a surprise, Mama. Don't look. I can do it."

Wanda didn't want to shatter his confidence, so she left him alone. Moments later, he said, "Come on. It's ready!"

Wanda stepped into the kitchen and gasped. There in the pot was the complete ration of tea. It was strong, muddy, and wasted. Instead of using a teaspoon to measure the tea, he had used a huge cooking spoon.

It was good to settle into the new accommodations before the weather got cold. As Christmas drew near, the older couple cut and decorated a small pine tree and placed it on their little table in front of the window. The tree was beautiful! It was decorated with puffs of cotton. Tied to the branches were colored clear candies wrapped in cellophane. The children longingly looked at the tree and hoped that some candy would be offered to them.

Although the table was just large enough to hold the Christmas tree, something amazing was placed beneath the tree. The children had never seen anything like it and wondered if it was real. It was a long, light object that looked like a loaf of bread. It was bread! It was a long white loaf of bread. Every loaf they had ever eaten was dark, coarse, and many times baked on sawdust, not at all like this angel white bread. It was a beautiful sight.

In preparation for Christmas, the couple spent many hours in the kitchen. Where they got the supplies for the goodies was a mystery. One of the delicacies they made was sausage. It was interesting to watch as the meat filled the casings and became sausage.

Wanda and her family never really celebrated Christmas during the war. Even before the war, not much fuss was made. As a child, Józef had nothing, so he felt that it was all right for his children to grow up without too much fuss. He believed toys were frivolous. If there were toys, Wanda bought them.

This Christmas was an especially nice one. A box arrived with a gift for each child and one for Wanda. It came from an aunt in America. She heard the good news that the family was alive and well, and promptly sent the gifts.

Romek received a flashlight, Danek a penknife, Ela a doll, and Wanda received beautiful embroidered handkerchiefs.

Ela was overjoyed. What a surprise, a gift for everyone. As she finished unpacking her gift, her smiles turned to tears. Her baby-size doll arrived with a shattered leg. Another casualty of war! "Never mind, dear," Wanda comforted. "I'll sew her a new leg." And so she did. One leg was made of a hard composite and the other of a soft cloth. Ela was satisfied.

Immediately, she went to the UNRA boxes and rummaged for clothing for her baby. She found small baby clothes and a little blanket made of wool. The blanket had three yellow chicks appliquéd on top and a few embroidered flowers. She did not know that the wool was shrunken. It did not matter. She was thrilled! To her, it was like finding something precious!

During the Christmas season, special food gifts were distributed from UNRA. Another wonderful box arrived with chocolate and orange juice concentrate, but along with that came Wanda's favorite treat, a package of smoked herring. What a luxurious treat! Everyone loved the smoked fish.

One morning as they rose and looked out the window, it was impossible for the boys to escape the beckoning of the newly fallen snow. Immediately, Romek and Danek put on their new second-hand winter hats, coats, and gloves and went outside to play. Finding other children, they built forts, had a snowball fight, and had a grand time chasing, laughing, and just being kids. It was exhilarating. As Romek played with the others, Danek wandered off by himself. There was so much to explore, so much to see. He was not satisfied to just stay in one place. He came upon a deep well. Leaning over, he shouted into the well and listened. Again, he shouted and enjoyed the echoing sound that returned to him. Again, he tried, but this time, something happened. His precious new, second-hand hat fell off his head and into the well. *Oh no, Mama will be angry,* he thought. *What shall I do? How can I get it?*

Without a second thought, he started climbing into the well, spread eagle. Down and down he went until he was at the bottom. A thin layer of ice cracked as he stepped on it, but thankfully, the water was every shallow. He reached for the hat and tucked it into his pocket.

Trying to climb up, he slipped. He slipped again. Going up was much harder than coming down. Again spread eagle, he tried climbing up. He kept slipping back down again. Who would find him if he stayed in the well? Who would rescue him? No one knew where he was. What could he do now? He did what his mother had taught him: *pray!* He prayed with intense zeal and sincerity. He prayed as he never had prayed before. Trying again and pushing against the sides, spread eagle, he slowly climbed. Little by little, he climbed until he reached the top.

When Danek arrived home, Wanda knew something was not right. "What happened to you?" Wanda asked as she looked at the flushed, scared face of her son.

"My hat fell down a well. I went after it but I couldn't get out. But Mama, I prayed like I never have before and God helped me." Wanda held him as he told the whole story.

The months passed quickly, and the family tried to be patient. When would they see Tata? When would the visas be ready? When would Tata come and get them?

At the end of January 1947, the news came. The visas were ready and Józef would arrive in a few days. Passage was booked on an ocean liner and they would leave for England early in February.

What excitement! What unrestrained excitement! The smiles just would not leave their faces.

"Wandzia! Oh, Wandzia! I never thought that I would see you again," Józef said as he embraced Wanda and lifted her off her feet. "Look at these children! Are these *my* children? I would never have recognized them. They are all so tall!" His eyes glazed over with tears as he tenderly looked at his children.

"Look, I have the visas," he said, waving them in the air. "We're going to England. It's wonderful there. You won't believe it! People walk around the streets in freedom. You can live and earn a living in peace. You'll love it."

Wanda just watched and smiled as the children danced around Józef with excitement and hope for the promised better life.

"We have so much to catch up on," Józef said as soon as they had some private time.

"Tell me, Józio, how did you get to the British zone? Tell me?" Wanda inquired. "How did you get away from the Nazis?"

"Shortly after I was drafted, our platoon was taken north to fight the British. It was horrible. I didn't want to be there and I certainly wasn't going to shoot a rifle. I've never shot a rifle, and I never will. I only held it and pretended so that they wouldn't put me in prison. I walked with the others and felt despicable the whole time.

"Over a loudspeaker the British announced, 'Any Pole who wants to come and join the British, drop your rifle and come now.'

"I wanted to go, but was afraid that my comrades would shoot me. I hesitated but then decided to run. I dropped my rifle and ran as fast as I could and expected to get shot in the back. As I got closer to the British, a British soldier ran out to help me. Just at that moment I turned around to see if anyone was chasing me. Instantly, the soldier got angry and jabbed me in the arm with his bayonet. He had a right to be angry. I could have caused both of us to get shot. In a split second, we both could have died.

"I bled like a pig. He dragged me to a medical unit and for some reason I blacked out and can't remember what happened. I lost my memory. I can't remember anything that happened for the next few weeks. They tell me that at first they took me to Scotland. From there I went to England, where my memory returned. I still can't remember everything.

"Now tell me, Wandzia, where were you? How was it for you? Tell me."

"Dear Józio. So much has happened since I last saw you. I can't even begin to tell you. Perhaps later! At another time I'll tell you. I just can't face it right now. When I think about it or talk about it, I'm not just remembering, I am there again. Maybe later, later I'll tell you."

Within days, the exciting trip started. From Bremerhaven the ship would sail to Southhampton, England. The children were so excited that they could hardly contain themselves.

Danek longed for the endless supply of ice cream; Romek, to see the captain.

Almost flying, they went up the ramp into the ship. The accommodations were exquisite. The cabin, just as Romek had imagined, had beds, one on top of the other (bunk beds). The walls, the furniture, the ceiling, everything was covered with beautiful polished wood. Even the commode in the lavatory was made of wood. What an amazing place.

When they got settled, they went to discover the dining room. Again, everything was far beyond expectations.

While Wanda and Józef talked, intently catching up on the past, and Ela and Danek were finishing their ice cream, Romek quietly left the table.

The waiter came to the table and politely said, "Would you like anything else?" Looking around, Wanda noticed that Romek was missing. Ignoring the waiter, she anxiously asked, "Where is Romek?"

Just then, Romek came dashing to the table, grinning from ear to ear and out of breath. "Mama, Tata, I met the captain! He *did* have a white uniform with gold buttons *and* he shook my hand!"

Wanda smiled and gave her son a big hug while Danek looked at the waiter, lifted two fingers, and said, "Two more scoops, please."

*Photo of Wanda, Józef and the children taken
just before leaving for England.*

Epilogue

September 28, 2007
SCREAM quietly
Elizabeth Carlson

After escaping from Poland, **Wanda** and her children reunited with her husband, Józef, and lived in England. In 1951 they immigrated to the United States. Wanda always worked long hours, had a second job on the weekends, and even cared for children in the evenings. Over the years, she loved to spend time in her garden and enjoyed painting in oils. She produced many beautiful paintings but always wished she had more time to paint. At age ninety five, Wanda continues to live in her home.

Romek, Wanda's oldest son, graduated from high school, attended college, and was drafted into the military. His military experience was unnerving. During a training exercise, he became terrified. He ran, screaming, as though he was in a war zone again, fleeing from the enemy. He was transferred into the medics and fulfilled his military obligation by vaccinating new enlistees. He passed away in 2002 after an accident.

Danek worked extremely long hours as a machinist, but always remained in good humor. He loved to joke around. He married and had three beautiful children, a son and two daughters. Although his memories of the early years never returned, he does not dwell on it. He prefers to live in the present and not recall the horror of the past. He is Wanda's primary caregiver.

Because **Czesia** was disabled, the Communist government did not grant her a visa. **Anna** stayed in Poland and cared for her daughter. They both passed away in Poland without ever again seeing Wanda and her children.

In 1960 **Zosia** immigrated to the United States with her daughter, Jagoda. They both learned to speak English and became productive, energetic, and happy citizens. Although Zosia was unable to find and reunite with her husband, the story did not end there. A few years before Zosia died, she was notified that **Leon** was alive and living in Germany. Although he had searched for his beloved wife and child, he never could find them. Before they could reunite, Leon passed away. He never remarried; instead, spent the years caring for his sister and her children. Zosia passed away in 1999.

Jagoda (Trudy) graduated from high school and married a tall, kind Texan and is enjoying a good life here in America. Just as Leon had invited Zosia's family to come and live with them, so Jagoda's husband invited Zosia to live in their home. The three of them had a happy and peaceful life together. Although Jagoda never saw her father, she can have sweet memories of him through the telling of this account. He was an exceptionally kind and good man.

After the war ended, **Bernard** was able to locate his wife and child. They remained in Poland and had two more children.

Wanda's husband, **Józef,** devoted his life to community projects and had great joy in helping immigrants resettle in America. Although he tried to forget, the terrors of war haunted him throughout his life. For the first time, at the age of eighty-two, he returned to Poland to visit old friends. While there, he died and was buried in Poland.

I am **Ela,** Wanda's youngest child. After graduating from college, I married my sweetheart, Stan. We lived in Germany while Stan served in the military. At a later date, a trip to Poland was a very emotional experience for me. I felt as though I was going to my death. I did not die and returned to live a life full of blessings. Blessings continually shower down on us through our precious daughter, son, their spouses, and our three grandsons. We are truly blessed.

It's still hard for me to believe that God was always with us, blessed us, and spared us from disaster time and time again. He continually cared for us, and still does – a simple, nothing special, ordinary type of family. Because He loves all of us so much, He even sent His Son, Jesus Christ to die for all our sins. All He wants us to do is believe and accept His sacrifice. We are amazingly blessed!

I pray that you, my friend, will continually look around and be aware of God and the wonderful blessings that He provides for you each day. The smallest and simplest things are not so small or simple when you no longer have them. Remember to thank God every day for His wonderful gifts.

God bless you, my friend, keep you safe, and may His face shine on you today and always. My prayer for you is that peace will surround you all the days of your life.

Elizabeth Carlson
(Ela)